Stress-Free Communication Skills for Couples

How to Recognize & Effectively Address Issues, Build Trust, and Resolve Conflicts for a Stronger Marriage or Relationship

By Sophia Simone

Contents

Chapter One

Embark on Your Journey Today!

T his workbook serves as a guide for couples looking to enhance
their romantic relationships through practical techniques that
foster intimate connections. It is essential to understand and be understood by your partner, using both verbal communication and body
language to express vulnerability regarding your thoughts and feelings. Building trust and reigniting passion are key components of this
process.

What sets this workbook apart is its interactive nature. It includes
games and reflective exercises that make the experience both informa-
tive and enjoyable.

As you progress through this workbook, you will experience enhanced
communication, deeper emotional connections, and revitalized intimacy.
Your commitment to this process is essential; the more you invest in the
growth of your relationship, the more rewarding your love will become.
Remember, your dedication is the cornerstone of this workbook's success.
Approach each chapter with an open mind and be ready to explore new
perspectives and ideas. Embrace this opportunity for growth, as your will-

ingness to adopt new ways of thinking and being is critical to achieving meaningful results.

Without further ado, let's get started! In this journey, we will explore the depths of emotional and sexual intimacy, reveal the secrets to lasting love, build trust, and rediscover intimacy. Your adventure awaits, and I am excited to guide you on this transformative path.

Bonuses

I truly appreciate you grabbing a copy of my book!
Just scan this QR code to access your exciting interactive workbook!

Unlock the valuable bonuses and interactive guide content that will significantly enhance your book. Take advantage of these essential resources:

Engage in additional activities designed specifically for couples, adding a fun twist to your relationship journey. Download the app for the convenience of independently completing activities on your phone, then compare your results with your partner to spark meaningful discussions.
Print out the questions, answer them thoughtfully, and have deep conversations about your responses.

Don't overlook these resources—they are crucial for accelerating your learning and taking your relationship to the next level! Use the app for independent activities, print out the questions for deep conversations, and engage in additional activities designed specifically for couples to reignite your spark. Together, they provide a comprehensive approach to relationship improvement.

Chapter Two

Secrets to Lasting Love

You need honest, direct, and courteous communication to cultivate emotional intimacy and connection in your relationship. When you want to bond with someone these are the key steps you should be taking:

1. Learn to Communicate Well: Express your emotions and concerns.

2. Prioritize Quality Time Together: Commit to setting aside dedicated time for each other, whether going out for dinner, taking walks, or engaging in shared hobbies.

3. Embrace Honesty: Be fully transparent with one another. This creates a secure environment where both partners can thrive.

4. Be There For One Another: Be empathetic and encouraging.

5. Express Appreciation Regularly: Acknowledge and value your partner's efforts. This fosters a more profound connection that should not be overlooked.

6. Use Physical Affection: Make it a point to engage in simple gestures like holding hands, hugging, or cuddling .

7. Resolve Conflicts Respectfully: Face conflicts head-on with respect and understanding and collaboratively seek solutions.

How can you successfully incorporate these practices into your daily routine?

Addressing these ideas can help you build a lasting relationship. Over time, a few small, regular things will show that you care and appreciate your spouse. Please don't put this off any longer; your relationship deserves it.

Expressing Needs: Share what you need to feel closer. For Example: *"I feel most connected when we spend quality time together without distractions."*

Nonverbal Communication: Use physical touch, facial expressions, and gestures to convey care and love. For example, a gentle touch on the shoulder can say, *"I'm here for you."*

Express Gratitude: Make it a point to share one thing you appreciate about your partner every single day. For instance, say, *"Thank you for making my coffee this morning—it really made my day easier."*

Show Physical Affection: Prioritize hugs, kisses, and holding hands to foster closeness. A quick hug before leaving for work can set a positive tone for the entire day.

Check-In Briefly: Make it a habit to ask about each other's day or emotions. For example, *"What was the highlight of your day today?"* This keeps you engaged with each other's lives.

Spend Quality Time: Dedicate 10-15 minutes to connecting without distractions. Enjoy a cup of tea together—no phones or TV interruptions allowed.

Active Listening: Demonstrate that you genuinely listen by summarizing your partner's words or asking clarifying questions. For example, say, *"It sounds like you're stressed about work. How can I support you?"*

Share Vulnerabilities: Open up about your fears, dreams, and challenges to build trust. For example, express, *"I've been feeling overwhelmed lately and could really use your support."* This invites intimacy.

Avoid Assumptions: Make it a rule to clarify rather than assume intentions. For instance, ask, *"Can you help me understand why you made that decision?"* instead of jumping to conclusions.

Celebrate Successes Together: Acknowledge each other's achievements to strengthen positivity in your relationship. For example, say, *"I'm so proud of how you handled that presentation!"*

Now, reflect on your current relationship. Assess how communication impacts your emotional closeness and which daily habits currently strengthen your bond. Identify adjustments that could enhance your connection further. What can you improve? Consider adding small actions that can further reinforce your connection.

Addressing Common Barriers to Intimacy

Identifying and tackling barriers to intimacy is crucial to resolving underlying issues that create distance between partners.

1. Life's stressors significantly reduce emotional availability, which is the ability to be present and responsive to your partner's emotional needs. Solution: Prioritize intentional time for relaxation and meaningful connection.

2. Lingering disagreements create emotional barriers. Solution: It's empowering to address conflicts decisively and respectfully, preventing them from festering and strengthening the relationship.

3. A fear of rejection or judgment blocks deeper intimacy. Solution: Share your feelings openly and reassure each other of unwavering support.

4. Relationships often fall into monotonous routines that kill excitement. Solution: Introduce novelty by exploring new activities such as hiking, cooking classes, or volunteering together. Surprise each other with thoughtful gestures like a handwritten note, a small gift, or a planned date night.

Take a moment to think about how you and your partner can actively tackle any potential obstacles that may arise. Explore strategies you can use to collaborate effectively and turn challenges into opportunities for growth together!

Chapter Three

Create and Foster Intimacy

This longing for reconnection is not uncommon; it's a universal challenge in relationships where closeness has eroded. Consider a couple that, much like many others, has drifted apart over time. Once filled with life and spontaneity, their discussions have become monotonous, revolving solely around bills and household chores, while date nights have vanished from their agenda. However, beneath this dull routine lies a powerful yearning for connection and a rekindling of the intimacy that once brought them immense joy.

Emotional intimacy is the essential pulse of a thriving relationship. Truly knowing your partner and being known in return elevates a partnership beyond mere cohabitation. Achieving this level of intimacy demands intentional effort and commitment, especially in our fast-paced world where time is scarce.

The rewards of investing in your relationship are profound and transformative. Relationships grounded in emotional intimacy form the bedrock of commitment and love, making them essential for any healthy partnership. Let's explore the significant impact of cultivating this deep connection on relationships.

Why Emotional Intimacy Matters?

Emotional intimacy is sharing thoughts, emotions, and weaknesses with a partner without judgment or dismissal. It's when two hearts unite in a concert of sympathy and acceptance. This essential part of a relationship creates trust, improves communication, and strengthens the relationship in general.

1. Strengthens the Bond: Closeness connects partners through shared experiences and creates resilience in facing challenges.

2. Enhances Communication: Intimacy allows open expression of needs and concerns, preventing misunderstandings and fostering collaboration.

3. Boosts Relationship Satisfaction: Research shows that emotional closeness is linked to greater relationship satisfaction and longevity.

4. Promotes Personal Growth: An emotionally intimate relationship offers unconditional support for partners to express their identities and explore self-knowledge.

To enhance emotional intimacy in your relationship, reflect on these key elements:

Trust is The Foundation—Emotional intimacy is founded on trust. Knowing that your partner will look out for you and not leave you hanging is comforting and provides a sense of security.

Vulnerability is The Key - When partners reveal their fears, dreams, and insecurities, they can get to know each other better and connect more deeply.

Empathy is The Bridge - Empathy is the bridge that connects partners on a deeper level, opening up the channel of knowledge and understanding necessary for emotional intimacy.

Active Listening is The Tool—Active listening, without judgment and with complete attention, is decisive for showing respect and concern and fostering a sense of being heard and understood in the relationship.

Overcoming Obstacles to Emotional Intimacy

Emotional intimacy offers significant rewards for couples, and achieving that deep connection is essential. Many partners will face challenges on their journey to true closeness, but it is crucial to push through these obstacles. Opening up may be difficult due to past traumas or insecurities, but sharing and building trust will effectively overcome these barriers. Communication and compromise are not optional; they are essential for couples seeking varying levels of emotional intimacy. The pressures of modern life cannot rob us of this essential connection. Make time for each other—it's imperative if you want to foster emotional closeness.

4 Ways to Enhance Your Emotional Closeness:

1. Embrace Open Communication: Foster an environment where both partners can share their thoughts and feelings freely, without fear of judgment. This lays the foundation for trust and understanding.

2. Express Appreciation: Regularly acknowledge and thank your partner for their presence and the little things they do. This not only strengthens your bond but also boosts their self-esteem.

3. Create Shared Experiences: Explore new activities together or engage in hobbies that you both enjoy. These experiences can reveal different facets of your personalities and deepen your connection.

4. Be Truly Present: When you're together, make a conscious effort to be fully engaged. Put away distractions and focus on your partner, showing them that they are your priority.

The Question Game

This game is a vital and engaging activity for couples, where participants take turns asking and answering questions to enhance their understanding of one another. It demands vulnerability, curiosity, and connection. The primary objective of the game is to cultivate intimacy by enabling partners to discover each other's thoughts, dreams, and feelings in a playful yet purposeful way.

Instructions: Choose a quiet, comfortable space to focus on each other without distractions. Optional: Light candles, play soft music, or pour a drink to make the environment more romantic. You can use the questions below or develop your own. Mix serious, thoughtful questions with light-hearted or playful ones. One partner asks a question, and the other answers. Then, switch roles. Encourage honesty and active listening. Avoid interrupting or judging.

Dig Deeper: If an answer sparks curiosity, ask follow-up questions to explore further. Example: *"Why is that memory so meaningful to you?"* or *"What inspired that dream?"* Play Until Satisfied: Set a timer (e.g., 20–30 minutes) or keep playing until you feel connected.

30 Questions for Building Emotional Intimacy

This collection of questions is a powerful mix of fun, romance, and reflection. A copy of this book provides insight into the content of the questions. To achieve the best results, make sure to utilize the bonus materials. You can print the questions, leaving space for both partners to answer, or use your mobile device to read and type your responses. When you're together, compare your answers, gain deeper insights into each other, and rekindle your love!

What's a dream you've never shared with me?

What would it be if you could relive one moment in our relationship?

What's a quirky habit of mine that you secretly love?

What's one thing about our relationship that makes you proud?

If you could describe me in three words, what would they be?

What's a silly memory of us that always makes you laugh?

If money weren't an issue, what would be your ideal date with me?

What's something small I do that makes your day better?

Where would it be if we could travel anywhere in the world together?

What's one thing you admire about me that I may not know?

How do you feel most supported by me?

What's one of your happiest childhood memories?

If you could learn a new skill, what would it be and why?

What's a fear or insecurity you've never shared with anyone else?

What's the best gift I've ever given you, and why?

How do you feel when I [specific action, like "hold your hand"]?

What's one thing you'd like us to do together more often?

What's a quality of mine that you hope never changes

If you could live in any era or time, which would it be and why?

What's one way I can make you feel more loved?

What's your favorite compliment I've ever given you?

What's one adventure you'd love to go on together?

If you could switch lives with anyone for a day, who would it be and why?

What's your favorite thing about how we resolve disagreements?

What romantic gesture would you love for me to do for you?

What's a habit or routine you have that you cherish?

What moment in our relationship made you fall deeper in love with me?

What advice would you give your future self about love in a letter?

What's one thing you want to experiment with in our relationship?

How do you envision our relationship growing in the next 5 years?

Tips for Success:

- Be Honest: Answer authentically, even if it feels vulnerable.

- Be Curious: Listen genuinely and ask clarifying questions.

- Be Playful: Mix serious and light-hearted questions to keep it engaging.

- Be Supportive: Create a safe space for sharing.

Chapter Four

Boost your Physical Bonds

P hysical contact is crucial for fostering a healthy relationship. It extends beyond just eroticism or sexuality; it's about expressing love, trust, and a deep connection through touch and closeness. Intimacy cultivates connection, confidence, and a genuine sense of belonging when practiced thoughtfully. Physical closeness encompasses all forms of affectionate touch, ranging from hand-holding to sexual intimacy. It reflects needs, desires, and loyalty, often conveyed through acts of affection. This expression of closeness varies widely between couples, and it's important to understand and respect each other's individual preferences.

Physical closeness triggers the release of oxytocin, known as the **"love hormone,"** which cultivates trust and deepens bonds. Engaging in physical affection not only establishes a safe space where individuals can freely express vulnerability without fear of judgment, but also creates a sense of security in the relationship.

Physical touch communicates emotions that words often fail to convey, offering reassurance, comfort, or passion. Simple gestures like hugging or cuddling are crucial; they lower stress hormones and enhance overall well-being. More than that, they bring joy and excitement to the relationship. Additionally, consistent physical intimacy is necessary to sustain passion, excitement, and a sense of playfulness in any relationship. Don't underestimate the power of touch—it is fundamental to fostering and maintaining a healthy partnership.

Key Elements of Physical Intimacy

Emotional Safety - Physical intimacy thrives when both partners feel emotionally secure. Open communication, mutual respect, and trust lay the foundation for physical closeness. Emotional safety ensures that physical gestures feel meaningful and reciprocated.

Consent and Comfort—Mutual consent is a cornerstone of physical intimacy. Both partners should feel comfortable with the types of touch and gestures exchanged and respect each other's boundaries and preferences.

Non-Sexual Affection - Physical intimacy isn't just about sexual activity. Non-sexual gestures like holding hands, hugging, or cuddling—are equally crucial for nurturing connection and love.

Understanding and Adaptability—Physical intimacy evolves. Life transitions, such as pregnancy, illness, or aging, may require adjustments. Understanding and flexibility ensure that the physical connection remains strong despite changes.

Playfulness and Spontaneity - Keeping physical intimacy playful and spontaneous prevents it from becoming routine. A surprise hug, a stolen kiss, or a dance can reignite passion and joy.

In strong relationships, it is essential to acknowledge that physical intimacy can face significant challenges. Busy schedules, stress, unresolved conflicts, and health issues often act as barriers. Couples must address these challenges head-on through open communication and deliberate efforts to ensure they maintain a robust physical connection.

We will overcome those challenges with communication. It is essential to discuss our preferences, challenges and needs openly. We must dedicate time to be physically and emotionally present with each other. Seeking counseling or therapy is not a sign of weakness, but a proactive step that can provide us with practical strategies to navigate barriers to intimacy, instilling hope and optimism in our relationship.

Before diving into games and activities, reflecting on how you and your partner perceive physical intimacy is essential. Consider these questions:

How do I feel when my partner initiates physical affection?
What types of touch make me feel most connected and loved?
Are there any gestures I'd like to introduce or experience more often?
What physical gestures make my partner light up or feel reassured?

Discussing these reflections lays the groundwork for meaningful connection and ensures that the activities you engage in are aligned with your unique relationship. Building a solid foundation for physical intimacy requires mutual effort and intention. This involves creating a safe, loving environment and making time for each other. The activities aim to deepen your understanding of each other's needs and rekindle passion. By nurturing this essential aspect of love, you strengthen your bond and cultivate lasting closeness and joy.

Games and Activities for Enhanced Physical Intimacy

The objective of this game is to empower couples to deepen their physical intimacy by exploring and sharing gestures that foster love, connection, and closeness. This interactive experience, with its four rounds and engaging activities, offers a unique opportunity for couples to identify and practice meaningful physical gestures. By doing so, they can strengthen their bond and enhance their relationship.

In Round 1, we will delve into your unique physical language to uncover the touch and gestures that deeply resonate with each partner, fostering a sense of love and connection like never before.

Activity 1: Physical Affection Preferences – Take turns asking and answering these reflective questions to identify what physical gestures mean the most to each other.

Questions:

What physical gestures (e.g., holding hands, hugs, kisses) make you feel most loved?
How do you feel about public displays of affection? Are there certain gestures you enjoy or dislike?
What's one small physical action I could do more often to make you feel cherished?
How do you like to reconnect physically after a stressful day?
Is there a physical gesture from the early days of our relationship that you miss or want to bring back?

Bonus Action: Write down three physical gestures that mean the most to you. Exchange lists and discuss why these gestures are meaningful.

Activity 2: Gestures of the Day – Each partner chooses one physical gesture to try throughout the day, such as a kiss on the cheek, a back rub, or holding hands during a walk. Share how the gesture made you feel and whether it deepened your connection.

In Round 2, we will cultivate moments of physical closeness to intentionally enhance our physical intimacy and deepen our connection with one another.

Activity 1: Sensory Connection Exercise – This exercise encourages couples to focus on nonverbal communication and physical closeness. Sit facing each other and hold or place your hands on each other's shoulders. Look into each other's eyes for 2–3 minutes without speaking. Afterward, share what the experience felt like.

Activity 2: "Touch Time" Game – Set a timer for 5 minutes. One partner gives the other a nonsexual touch (e.g., a massage, tracing patterns on their arm, or playing with their hair). After the timer ends, switch roles. Discuss what types of touch felt most enjoyable or relaxing.

In Round 3, we aim to establish regular physical rituals that foster love and strengthen connections in your daily life. By incorporating these practices, you can create a nurturing environment that enhances your relationships and brings joy to your routine.

Activity 1: Build Your "Physical Intimacy Menu"—Together, brainstorm a list of physical gestures and actions you'd like to incorporate into your relationship.Examples: Morning hugs or goodnight kisses; holding hands during walks or drives; regular cuddling sessions; and surprise gestures, like a forehead kiss or an unexpected back rub. Choose 3–5 gestures from the list to practice consistently for a week.

Activity 2: Revisit "The Power of Firsts" – Think back to the early stages of your relationship. Identify physical gestures that felt special or significant, and recreate one of those moments. **Example**: If your first date involved walking hand in hand, plan a walk together and hold hands as you reminisce about that time.

In Round 4, we invite you to explore physical intimacy in a way that is both creative and enjoyable, transforming it into a natural and fulfilling aspect of your relationship. Embrace the fun and deepen your connection!

Activity 1: Playful Physical Challenge – Pick a fun, physical activity that involves closeness. Examples: For a dance challenge, Put on your favorite music and dance together in your living room. Try partner yoga poses that require teamwork and physical connection for a yoga session. Reflect on how engaging in playful touch or movement enhances your bond.

Activity 2: "Trust Touch" Challenge – One partner is blindfolded while the other gently guides them with physical touch (e.g., through a short walk, light movements, or gentle gestures). After 5 minutes, switch roles. Share how it felt to trust your partner and be guided by touch alone.

20 Questions for Building Physical Intimacy

Use these questions to spark meaningful conversations and discover what physical connection means to you and your partner.

What's your favorite type of physical touch, and why?

How do you feel about physical affection in public settings?

What's one small gesture that made you feel loved?

Are there times of day when you feel more open to physical connection?

How do you like to be comforted physically when you're upset?

What's a physical moment in our relationship that you'll never forget?

How has our physical intimacy changed since we first met?

What playful gesture that we've shared would you like to recreate?

When do you feel most physically connected to me?

What's one thing we used to do physically that you'd like to bring back?

How can I help you feel more comfortable sharing your physical needs?

Are there any physical gestures you wish I would try more often?

How do you feel when I initiate physical affection?

What's one way we can build more trust around physical intimacy?

What do you need from me to feel more physically connected?

What's a new physical activity we could explore together?

How can we prioritize physical closeness in our busy lives?

What's a romantic getaway or experience we could plan that would enhance our physical connection and bring us even closer together?

What would you want it to include in a "physical intimacy ritual"?

What's one playful physical activity you've always wanted to try together?

Outcome of the Physical Intimacy Challenge

Participating in this challenge is essential for couples looking to deepen their understanding of the physical gestures and actions that evoke feelings of love and connection. Physical intimacy will transform into a vital and cherished element of your partnership. By adopting creative and fun approaches, you will keep the physical connection vibrant and exhilarating.

Chapter Five

Navigate your Spiritual Life

S piritual intimacy is the key to a more prosperous and lasting relationship between partners. It is a deep connection not rooted exclusively in religious or spiritual beliefs but in shared values and a common mission. It is about finding meaning and depth in the relationship, and it can be developed through shared rituals and practices or by engaging in deep conversations about life's great questions.

Spiritual connection is about bonding to find common ground, resolving value conflicts, discerning the purpose of life, and helping you to move forward. For some, spiritual intimacy means meditating; for others, it could be engaging in shared hobbies or having deep conversations about their mission, beliefs, or the legacy they want to pass down.

Spiritual intimacy is essential as it promotes growth, strengthens resilience, and enriches our lives with deeper meaning. Embracing it can transform relationships and enhance our overall emotional well-being, it fosters personal growth, builds resilience, and enhances the meaning in our lives.

Aligning fundamental values such as kindness, gratitude, and generosity serves as the bedrock for a meaningful relationship. Respecting and actively supporting each other's unique spiritual journeys is non-negotiable. Engaging in shared practices—whether meditation, prayer, or nature walks—is crucial; these activities deepen your connection through purposeful engagement.

Key Elements Common Barriers to Spiritual Intimacy

Discussing profound questions that matter to both of you is vital. This exchange fosters growth and solidifies your bond. Additionally, collaborating on acts of service or pursuing shared goals that resonate with your values significantly strengthens spiritual intimacy.

It's important to acknowledge that differences in beliefs or approaches can arise even in the strongest relationships. The critical factor is how you navigate these differences: approach them with respect and curiosity. Embrace the challenge, as it can ultimately lead to a richer spiritual connection.

If you've ever felt like your spiritual connection with your partner could be stronger, you're not alone. Many couples face these common barriers, but with understanding and effort, they can be overcome.

We bridge our differences by actively asking questions about each other's beliefs and life experiences. This will lead to a deeper understanding and connection. We must set aside dedicated time for shared practices or meaningful discussions that promote growth for both individuals. It's essential to focus on the values and interests we share, as this strengthens our bond, even when our beliefs differ.

Before starting any activities, take a moment to reflect on what spiritual intimacy means to you and consider these crucial questions:

How do I define spirituality in my life and in our relationship?
What core values do we both cherish and prioritize together?
How can we collaborate to explore life's purpose and meaning?

Games and Activities for Spiritual Intimacy

Game 1 highlights the transformative power of shared values. By identifying and embracing these values, you can strengthen the meaning and purpose within your relationship.

Instructions: Each partner writes down five values they hold dear (e.g., kindness, gratitude, and courage). Then, they exchange lists and discuss overlaps and differences. Choose two to three values to prioritize in your relationship. Brainstorm ways to embody these values together.

Game 2, known as "The Legacy Jar," invites you to envision your shared aspirations and the impactful legacy you aim to build together as a couple.

Instructions: Grab a jar and some slips of paper. Write down answers to the following prompts:

"What do I want our relationship to be remembered for?"
"What's is one dream we can pursue together?"

Review each other's responses and discuss making these values a reality.

Game 3 creates a meaningful ritual that deepens your spiritual connection and enriches your bond.

Instructions: Brainstorm ideas for a ritual you can do together regularly. For example, you might share three things you're thankful for in your life, go on weekly nature walks to reflect on the beauty of life or hold meditation or prayer sessions for guidance and grounding. Try your chosen ritual for a month and evaluate its impact.

Game 4 prompts you to explore profound questions that spark truly impactful conversations, fostering a deeper understanding between you.

Instructions: Take turns answering thought-provoking questions. Reflect on each other's answers, focusing on understanding and curiosity. Examples: *"What do you think is our purpose as a couple?"*

"How do you find meaning during difficult times?"
"What" "does a fulfilling life look like to you?"
"What" role does spirituality play in your life?"

30 Questions for Building Spiritual Intimacy

How do you define spirituality in your life?

What role do faith, religion, or spirituality play in your daily routine?

What's your purpose during stressful times?

Is it a spiritual experience or moment that's deeply impacted you?

How do you see your spiritual journey evolving?

What values do you think are most important in our relationship?

How can we embody generosity in our daily lives?

What's one way we can bring more gratitude into our relationship?

How do you feel when we work together on a shared goal?

What legacy do you hope we leave behind?

What's one thing you're deeply grateful for in our relationship?

How do you feel discussing more significant questions?

What's a lesson you've learned recently that has strengthened our bond?

How can I support your spiritual or personal growth?

How do you feel about exploring new spiritual practices together?

What weekly ritual, we could introduce to strengthen our connection?

How can we make time for prayer in our busy lives?

What's one shared activity that could deepen our bond?

How do you feel about creating an affirmation practice together?

What's one way we can celebrate the beauty or mystery of life together?

How can we use our relationships to impact the world positively?

What's act of service we could do as a couple to align our values?

How can we support what others' dreams or callings are in life?

What long-term goal could we pursue that feels meaningful to us?

How can spirituality guide us through challenges as a couple?

How do you envision our journey as a couple in 5 years?

What's one tradition or practice we could pass on to future generations?

How can we continue growing in our understanding of life's more profound questions?

What does spiritual intimacy mean to you, and how can we nurture it?

How do you think our shared purpose will evolve as we grow older?

Spiritual intimacy is about creating a relationship that thrives on love and feels deeply connected to something greater than yourself. By engaging in these reflections, games, and practices, couples can cultivate a profound sense of unity and purpose.

Chapter Six

Build Stronger Bonds

Relational intimacy refers to the deep sense of closeness and collaboration that emerges when couples actively nurture their relationship as a partnership. It involves feeling seen, heard, and valued by interacting with and supporting each other. This intimacy strengthens a relationship's emotional and practical foundation, enabling couples to navigate challenges, celebrate joys, and grow together.

Compelling Reasons to Cultivate Relational Intimacy are:

1. Enhances Collaboration: Couples who nurture relational intimacy partner effectively to achieve common goals and navigate life's challenges. Working together to manage daily tasks and responsibilities is a practical necessity and a powerful way to strengthen the partnership and prevent resentment.

2. Fosters Emotional Security: A united front instills a profound sense of safety and stability within the relationship. Creating and pursuing shared goals ensures that both partners share the same vision for the future.

3. Boosts Communication: Relational intimacy paves the way for open and respectful conversations, enhancing understanding between partners. Sharing one's thoughts, feelings, and needs fosters understanding and builds trust.

4. Deepens Connections: Sharing experiences like traveling together, or responsibilities like managing household chores, strengthens the emotional bond, forging a closer partnership. Relational intimacy involves support during tough times and approaching problems as a team rather than as individuals.

5. Promotes Personal Growth: Supporting each other's aspirations and growth fosters a more prosperous, more fulfilling relationship. Acknowledging and celebrating achievements, big or small, is not just a feel-good exercise. It's a powerful tool that reinforces mutual respect and appreciation, making each partner feel valued and respected, and thereby strengthening the bond between them.

Even the strongest partnerships face obstacles that can strain relational intimacy. Unbalanced responsibilities, hectic schedules, differing priorities, lack of shared goals, and avoidance of conflict can lead to emotional distance. To strengthen the bond, it is essential to engage in proactive communication and make a deliberate effort to address these challenges.

Transforming Challenges in a Relationship

Prioritize meaningful conversations to effectively address concerns and strengthen your bond. Collaborate as a team and share responsibilities to foster unity and cooperation, ensuring both partners feel supported and valued. Celebrate your journey and accomplishments together; this not only brings joy but also reinforces your connection and commitment, giving you both a greater sense of security in your relationship. Tackling obstacles together is essential; take a shared approach to overcoming challenges and emerge stronger as a couple, knowing that you have each other's back. Before engaging in activities, reflect on how you perceive it:

What moments make you feel most connected to your partner as a team?
How do you and your partner share responsibilities or support each other?
What's one way your relationship could feel more balanced?

Games and Activities

Game 1: "Us vs. The Problem" empowers couples to unite in tackling challenges, highlighting the value of teamwork and collaboration.

Instructions: Identify a minor challenge or decision you must make together (e.g., planning a weekend activity, organizing a room, or deciding on a vacation spot). Approach the problem as a team, brainstorming solutions collaboratively. Reflect on how working together felt. What made it effective? What could be improved next time?

Game 2: The Shared Vision Collage is a creative way to visualize and articulate your shared goals and dreams, fostering unity.

Instructions: Gather supplies (magazines, scissors, glue, paper) or use a digital tool like Canva. Create a collage of words, images, and symbols representing your shared dreams (e.g., travel, financial goals, personal growth). Display the collage in a visible spot as a reminder of your shared vision.

Game 3: Strengths and Superpowers encourages you to celebrate and value each other's unique contributions, enhancing appreciation in your relationship.

Instructions: Each partner writes down 3–5 strengths or "superpowers" they see in the other (e.g., patience, creativity, problem-solving). Share your lists and discuss how these qualities enhance your relationship. Reflect on leveraging each other's strengths to tackle future challenges.

Game 4: Regular relationship evaluations encourage open communication and provide opportunities to strengthen your bond and connection.

Instructions: Schedule a 20-minute check-in each week. Answer these prompts together:

What went well in our relationship this week?
What could we improve as a team?
How can I support you better in the coming week?
What's one thing you're grateful for in our relationship?

30 Questions for Building Relational Intimacy

What's one way we make a great team?

How do you feel about how we share responsibilities in our relationship?

What's a decision we made together that you're proud of?

How do we handle challenges as a couple?

How have we grown more potent as a team over time?

What's an achievement that you feel we haven't celebrated enough?

How do you feel when I acknowledge your efforts?

What's a small win we've had recently that you're proud of?

How can we better celebrate each other's accomplishments?

What's one success you'd like to aim for together in the next year?

What's a dream we've talked about that you're excited to achieve?

How do you see our relationship evolving in the next 5 years?

What's a shared goal we still need to set that you'd like to discuss?

How do you feel about balancing individual and shared goals?

What's one adventure or experience you'd like to have together?

What's one thing I do that makes you feel supported as a partner?

How can we improve our communication about daily tasks?

What's a routine or habit we could introduce to feel more connected?

How could I make you feel more appreciated in our relationship?

How can we make our relationship feel more balanced or collaborative?

What do you think about how we handle disagreements or conflicts?

What's one area of our relationship where you feel we could grow stronger?

What's a challenge we've faced recently that you think we handled well?

How can we better support each other during stressful times?

What's one thing we could work on together to better our relationship?

What's a shared ritual we could create to strengthen our connection?

How can we make time for each other despite busy schedules?

What's one way we can keep our relationship fun and exciting?

How can we stay connected even during difficult periods?

What's one small action I can take to help you feel more supported daily?

Relational intimacy isn't just about managing tasks or setting goals—it's about building a partnership where love, respect, and connection thrive.

Chapter Seven

Grow Together Intellectually

Intellectual intimacy is the powerful bond that emerges between couples as they discuss ideas, discover hobbies, and engage in intellectually stimulating conversations. It's about collaboration, questioning, and appreciating each other's ideas. This intimacy is vital for maintaining and evolving a relationship's integrity, making each person more deeply connected and understood. It's not about always agreeing but respecting each other's viewpoints. More importantly, intellectual closeness catalyzes mutual growth and a curious outlook toward the world. This can bring a new dimension to your relationship, full of potential and hope.

Five Compelling Reasons to Nurture Intellectual Intimacy

1. Encourages Personal Growth: Exchanging ideas helps both partners evolve individually and in a communication relationship. Activities that challenge both partners intellectually cultivate a profound sense of connection.

2. Enhances Communication: Thought-provoking discussions foster a deeper understanding and mutual respect. Intellectual intimacy flourishes through open conversations characterized by sharing thoughts, attentive listening, and embracing differences.

3. Stimulates Curiosity: A mutual passion for exploration and learning injects excitement into the relationship. Being curious about each other's thoughts, interests, and perspectives elevates the relationship dynamic.

4. Cultivates respect: Appreciating each other's ideas establishes a foundation of trust and admiration. Engaging in healthy debates and being open to challenging each other's points promote more profound understanding and reinforce bonds of trust.

5. Improves Problem-Solving: Intellectual intimacy empowers couples to tackle challenges together with creativity. Supporting each other fosters teamwork and mutual respect, leading to innovative solutions.

Nurturing Intellectual Intimacy

Intellectual intimacy is often sidelined, primarily due to varying interests or hectic lifestyles. Yet, acknowledging its significance and prioritizing time for deep mental connections can effectively address these hurdles. Key challenges include mismatched interests, limited time, and the anxiety surrounding potential disagreements.

To cultivate intellectual intimacy, couples should explore topics or activities that ignite passion in both partners. Carving out time for meaningful discussions and embracing intellectual differences as opportunities for mutual growth can significantly enhance the bond. Before diving into activities, reflect on your intellectual connection:

What topics or ideas excite me, and how can I share them with my partner?
How do I feel when my partner engages with my thoughts and interests?
What's one way we can foster curiosity and learning together?

Games and Activities for Intellectual Intimacy

Game 1: "Big Questions" Challenge – Immerse yourselves in thought-provoking questions to ignite stimulating conversations and deepen your connection.

Instructions: Take turns answering these questions, share follow-up thoughts and discuss what you learned from each other's answers.

"What's a book, movie, or idea that changed how you think about the world?"
"What's one thing you've always wanted to learn more about?"
"If you could solve one global problem, what would it be and why?"

Game 2: Learn Something New Together – Embark on a shared intellectual adventure, fostering a powerful bond.

Instructions: Choose a topic or skill you'd like to learn together (e.g., nature, history, coding, or philosophy). Dedicate time each week to exploring it—through classes, documentaries, or reading. Please share what you've learned and discuss how it applies to your lives or relationships.

Game 3: Debate Night – Cultivate an open mind and respect for differing viewpoints through engaging dialogue.

*Instructions:*Pick a light-hearted or thought-provoking topic (e.g., "Is creativity more important than logic?"). Each partner takes a side, regardless of personal belief, and presents their argument. Afterward, switch sides to explore the other perspective. Discuss what you learned from each other.

Game 4: The Dream Journal – Collaborate on your aspirations and intellectual ambitions to create a shared vision for the future.

Instructions: Write down your intellectual goals or dreams (e.g., writing a book, mastering a skill, starting a project). Share your lists and brainstorm ways to support each other in achieving these goals. Choose one shared dream to work on together.

32

30 Intellectual Intimacy Questions

What's a topic or subject you're passionate about, and why?

What's one thing you've learned recently that excited or inspired you?

How do you like to challenge yourself intellectually?

What's a book, article, or podcast that you think I'd enjoy?

What's a skill or hobby you've always wanted to learn?

What's a belief or value that has shaped the way you think?

If you could ask any historical figure a question, who would it be and what would you ask them?

What's one big question about life that you'd love to explore together?

How do you feel about the balance between AI and creativity?

What's your favorite way to engage in thought-provoking conversations

What's a time when we learned something together that brought us closer?

How can I better support your intellectual interests or goals?

What's one thing we could explore to deepen our intellectual connection?

What challenge or problem have we solved that made you proud of us?

How can we use our differences in thinking to strengthen our relationship?

What ritual or habit could we start engaging intellectually as a couple?

How can we balance light-hearted fun with intellectual conversations?

How can we encourage each other to stay curious and open-minded?

How do you feel about discussing current events or controversial topics?

How can we bring more creativity or exploration into our routine?

If we could create a project together, what would it be?

What shared intellectual goal would strengthen our bond?

How do you envision our intellectual connection as we grow older?

What would it be if we could spend a day learning something new?

How can we leave a legacy of learning or curiosity for others?

What's an experience we've shared made you feel closer to me?

How can we encourage each other to grow in areas we're passionate about?

What subject or idea should we explore together more deeply?

How do you think intellectual intimacy influences our relationship?

What's one new tradition we could create to prioritize intellectual growth?

Intellectual intimacy allows couples to connect through their minds, fostering a deeper bond built on mutual respect, curiosity, and shared growth. These activities and discussions provide the tools to cultivate a relationship that's not only loving but also mentally enriching and inspiring.

Chapter Eight

Create Intimacy Rituals

I ntimacy rituals are crucial for a lasting relationship, especially during busy and stressful times. They build confidence, calm your partner, and consistently remind you of your love and care. Regular physical touch and tender gestures reignite passion and keep the flame alive. These rituals are potent tools that demonstrate the depth of your love and commitment, ensuring your relationship remains vibrant and resilient.

They aim to build stable routines that help couples develop emotional and physical closeness through individualized rituals. Sexual rituals are intentional habits or practices that couples perform together regularly to support intimate proximity, physical bonding, and relationship development. They can be as simple as a daily hug or as complex as a monthly date night ritual.

How to Create Intimacy Rituals

Step 1: Identify Your Intimacy Needs. Reflect on what intimacy means to both of you. Discuss which areas of intimacy feel strong and identify those that may need more attention.

Step 2: Brainstorm Ideas Together. Consider simple actions or activities that help you feel loved and connected. For instance, you could share a gratitude practice before bedtime, schedule a weekly date night, start the day with a kiss or cuddle, and regularly express verbal affirmations or compliments.

Step 3: Start Small. Implement one or two rituals, focusing on consistency over complexity. For example, "Let's spend 10 minutes discussing our day without distractions every evening."

Step 4: Make It Personal. Tailor rituals to your relationship. Use shared interests, hobbies, or unique quirks as inspiration. For example, if you love music, create a weekly playlist together and dance in your room.

Step 5: Evaluate and Adjust. Check regularly to see how the rituals are going. Are they helping you connect? Do they need tweaking? As your relationship evolves, add new rituals.

It's time to experience profound connections and cultivate intimacy with these powerful rituals. Embrace unique combinations that enhance your relationships and build lasting bonds.

Strengthen Connection Through Emotional Intimacy Rituals

Daily Check-In: Spend 10 minutes each evening sharing the highs and lows of your day.
Gratitude Practice: Share one thing you're grateful for about your partner each night.
Couple Journaling: Write in a weekly shared journal about your relationship goals, memories, or dreams.

Elevate Physical Intimacy with Engaging Rituals

Morning Affection: Start the day with a hug, kiss, or back rub.
Date Nights: Dedicate one night a week to reconnect physically and emo-

tionally without distractions.
Evening Wind-Down: Spend 15 minutes cuddling before bed, focusing on touch and connection.

Discover Innovative Combination Rituals

Adventure Rituals: Plan a monthly outing or try a new activity together.
Annual Vision Board: Create a shared vision board of your dreams and goals each year.
"Pause and Play": Use a playful gesture (like a kiss or inside joke) to reset connection during stressful times.

30 Intimacy Ritual Questions

What daily habits could we introduce to make us feel closer emotionally?

How can we better express our gratitude for each other?

What's one thing we could do regularly to make each other laugh?

How can we create a safe space to share our feelings without judgment?

What words or phrases make you feel most loved and supported?

How can we show kindness to each other, even on busy or stressful days?

What's one small way we can celebrate our relationship regularly?

What would be the best way during the day to show you how much I care?

What's our memory that we could turn into a ritual (e.g. a first date)?

How can we make time for meaningful conversations weekly?

What type of physical affection do you value most (e.g., hugs, kisses)?

How can we prioritize physical touch in our daily lives?

Would you enjoy a ritual of a goodnight kiss or cuddling before bed?

How do you feel about scheduling regular intimate weekends?

What's one way we can make our physical connection more playful?

How can we be more present with each other?

What's one way I can publicly show you affection that you'd enjoy?

How would you like to reconnect physically after a disagreement?

What sensory experiences make physical intimacy more enjoyable?

How can we create a way to show physical closeness when apart?

What's a weekly or monthly activity we could do together?

How can we create a ritual that helps us relax and unwind as a couple?

What's a shared interest or hobby we could turn into a regular activity?

How can we make our mealtimes more intentional and intimate?

Would you enjoy watching the sunset, stargazing, or having a picnic?

How could we use anniversaries to create meaningful traditions?

What's one way we can start or end each day together that feels special?

What does a perfect "day of connection" look like for you?

How can we use technology to maintain connection when apart?

How can we keep learning about each other, even after years together?

Regular rituals are essential for developing closeness habits that significantly strengthen emotional and physical bonds. These rituals establish crucial moments of stability and comfort, creating a nurturing environment that effectively reduces stress and enhances the relationship. Consistent acts of care and connection are vital for bolstering trust and emotional safety, ensuring that both partners feel secure and reassured in their relationship.

Rituals also carve out intentional spaces for open sharing and active listening, empowering both partners and transforming communication into a powerful tool for deepening intimacy. Physical rituals, with their role in reigniting the spark and sustaining ongoing desire, infuse excitement and invigoration into the relationship, making partners feel passionate about each other. Ultimately, these rituals act as anchors of love, equipping partners to confidently navigate life's challenges.

Chapter Nine

The Power of Empathy

E mpathy, the magic that draws humanity into the bonds of human connection, is a skill we should strive to master in our relationships. But what is empathy, and what does it tell us about our relationship with others? Let's talk about the impact that emotional intelligence can make on relationships and what good it can do. Empathy is imagining oneself in another's position—not just sympathy. It is about being able to relate to and empathize with someone else. This emotional intensity, especially in a relationship, allows couples to bond over everything that happens.

Why Empathy Matters?

Empathy is essential for strengthening emotional bonds and enhancing communication. When partners actively practice empathy, they create an environment that fosters vulnerability and authenticity—cornerstones of a robust and lasting relationship.

Empathetic listening goes beyond merely hearing words; it involves grasping the emotions and motivations behind them. This elevated level of communication empowers partners to avoid misunderstandings and resolve conflicts swiftly and effectively. By consistently demonstrating empathy, couples clearly communicate their respect for each other's feelings and thoughts. This respect builds trust, an indispensable element of a thriving marriage.

How to Cultivate Empathy in Your Relationship?

Empathy takes time and effort to learn. What can you do to achieve it? Give your partner your full attention when they speak. Listen to their opinion rather than trying to formulate your own. If your partner is upset about a work situation, imagine how you would feel in their position. This will give you a natural edge in empathy.

Spend time talking openly about what you feel. Create a nonjudgmental environment in which both partners feel comfortable speaking their minds. This can be done by setting aside specific times to discuss feelings and actively listening without interrupting or judging. In disputes, you should be able to understand your partner and respond clearly and kindly to their emotions.

Empathy is an essential and powerful tool for effectively resolving conflicts. Embracing conflicts from an empathic perspective allows you to de-escalate tense situations, find common ground with less effort, and create solutions that reflect the needs of both partners. Once you learn to empathize in your relationship, you might see its positive effects extend outside.

9 Workbook Questions

Practice with those Perspective-taking questions. The questions are designed to help each partner understand the other's feelings, experiences, and perspectives. Take turns asking and answering. The listening partner should focus on understanding and validating their partner's response.

What's one thing I do that makes you feel the most loved?

How has our relationship changed you in ways you didn't expect?

What's something small we could do daily to keep the spark alive?

What's a secret fantasy or dream you've never shared with me?

What's something that's been weighing on you lately, and how can I support you?

If you describe how you're feeling this week in one word, what would it be and why?

How can I help you feel more understood in our relationship?

When was the last time you felt genuinely heard by me, and what made it meaningful?

What's a decision you've made recently that you feel I haven't fully understood?

Follow-up Prompt for the Listener: *"I'd like to understand more about what led to that decision."*

Empathy makes interactions with loved ones, friends, and coworkers more comfortable. You can create a more harmonious work environment by understanding and respecting their feelings. Remember that this empathic growth takes time, but the rewards in more rewarding relationships are immeasurable.

Make a Difference with Your Review

USA REVIEW PAGE

"Great opportunities to help others seldom come, but small ones surround us every day."-- Sally Koch

Giving without expecting anything back makes our lives brighter and helps others in ways we might never see. Right now, you have a chance to do just that. **Will you help someone you don't know if it costs you nothing and you don't get credit for it?**

That "someone" could be a person who feels stuck, worried, or confused about how to talk with their partner. They might need this book to find hope and new ideas. But first, they must see that this book is worth their time. That's where your review can help.

Your Review Makes a Significant Difference

Most people look at a book's cover and reviews before reading it. By sharing your thoughts, you can guide others and show them how this book can improve their relationships. Your review could be the deciding factor for someone needing this book, making you a powerful influencer in their decision-making process. **Leaving a review is a quick and easy way to**

43

make a difference. It takes less than 60 seconds, but its impact can last a lifetime. Your contribution, though small in time, is significant and valuable.

Your honest feedback might inspire someone you'll never meet. You can leave your review on popular bookstores or websites like Amazon or Goodreads. Click the link below to leave your review. Even a few words can mean the world to someone searching for better communication methods. Please take a moment to leave your review now.

UK REVIEW PAGE

If you enjoy helping a stranger just by sharing your thoughts, welcome to the club! I appreciate your support in spreading the word about "Stress-Free Communication Skills for Couples:"

Thank you so much for being part of this mission. Now, let's return to learning how to build closer, happier partnerships—one simple step at a time.

Your biggest fan, **Sophia Simone**

P.S. Sending a copy of this book to someone who needs it is another way to share kindness. It might be the start of a positive change in their life.

P.P.S. If you want your review to stand out, consider adding a photo—maybe the cover or a favorite page. Your picture and a few words of praise can touch the hearts of many. Thank you for being part of this journey!

Chapter Ten

Strength of Vulnerability

V ulnerability, often overlooked, is a powerful catalyst for love and
friendship. It's not a weakness but a tool for forged, unbreakable
bonds and true intimacy. We'll explore how vulnerability can revolutionize
relationships and how you can nurture it. Vulnerability is the willingness
to let others see who you are in your fear, desire, and imperfections. When
it comes to the love life, vulnerability is an expression of emotional openness, risk, openness of speech, and belief in yourself and your partner.
Couples who are vulnerable establish the basis for authentic, life-long
connections. It's not a one-sided act. Both partners must be open and
honest, creating a culture of mutual understanding.

Benefits of Embracing Vulnerability

By being vulnerable, partners reap many advantages: Enhanced trust and
intimacy, forming deeper emotional bonds, increased understanding and
empathy, authenticity in self-expression, and individual development and
friendship. These benefits keep a relationship healthy and stable, making
it a place where love can flourish.

Vulnerability is a fundamental component of personal growth and should not be underestimated. You can conquer the fear of rejection, judgment, and appearing weak by sharing personal anecdotes, practicing mindfulness to maintain a presence, affirming your confidence in your relationships, and engaging in guided vulnerability exercises. You have the power to face these fears head-on and evolve.

By actively working on these skills, partners will become more comfortable with vulnerability, creating a strong sense of support and connection in their personal growth journey. Embrace the process and watch your relationships thrive.

Practical Strategies for Cultivating Vulnerability

Take these steps to make your relationship vulnerable:
Give yourself time dedicated to open discussions.
Create a private and safe environment for personal interactions.
Create rituals that encourage the opening up of one's thoughts and emotions.
Practice empathy and non-judgmental responses.
Give gratitude to your partner's weakness regularly.

By bringing these practices into daily life, couples can become vulnerable to one another as part of their intimacy. In the end, vulnerability requires courage and faith. When both partners become vulnerable, the relationship is stable against obstacles, exciting emotionally on many levels, built on respect and understanding, and ready to change and expand with time.

20 Questions to Start the Conversation

What's a fear you've never told anyone about?

What thing would you share with me so I can understand you better?

What's a moment from your past that still makes you feel vulnerable?

If there's something you've always hesitated to tell me, what is it?

What mistake have you made that you still wish to forgive yourself for?

What would it be if you could let go of one worry or insecurity right now?

What's about our relationship that you're afraid to say out loud?

What's a childhood memory that shaped who you are today?

What if you could ask me anything without fear of being judged?

What's one way you'd like me to support you more emotionally?

What have you never shared with anyone out of fear of their reaction?

What is a moment in our relationship when you felt truly understood?

What would it be if you could express one hidden hope for our future?

What's a part of yourself you've been scared to show me?

What's a question you wish I'd ask you, but I never have?

What's a time you felt genuinely vulnerable, and how did you handle it?

If there's one thing you've always needed to hear from me, what is it?

How could I make you feel safer sharing your feelings with me?

What's an insecurity you have that you wish I could understand better?

If there's one thing you've been holding back, what will it be?

Asking these questions encourages openness and cultivates a safe, meaningful conversation between partners. The bottom line is that vulnerability is not a vice but a virtue that can alter relationships. Vulnerability is a high cliff climb, but it is worth the struggle. If couples try it, they can live more authentically, robustly, and heartwarmingly.

Chapter Eleven

Build Lasting Trust

I t's not possible to compromise on trust in a romantic relationship. It's the bedrock where both partners can be secure, respected, and appreciated. If you want to build trust, you need to open up. Be honest about what you think and feel and consistent with what you say and do.

Resolving conflicts with empathy, not accusation, is a humane approach that makes both partners feel understood and valued. This leads to reconciliation, fostering forgiveness and healing, which are the keys to building trust. By investing in honesty, confidence, and empathy, you can form a solid relationship in the long run. Trust is not just desirable, it's the basis of deep love.

How to Foster Trust in Relationships?

Building trust in relationships begins with open and honest communication, which is the cornerstone of any strong partnership. When both parties engage in transparent dialogue, even about complex subjects such as financial issues, personal insecurities, or past traumas, they can effectively navigate challenges together.

Recognizing and honoring each person's unique needs and limitations demonstrates genuine care and consideration, reinforcing the trust that binds you. Over time, trust is cultivated through consistent actions; when your behavior aligns with your words, it brings much-needed stability to the relationship.

Indicators of a Trustworthy Relationship

Partners feel free to express their thoughts without fear of misinterpretation. Conflicts are addressed constructively, focusing on resolution rather than blame. Both individuals feel secure sharing their dreams and vulnerabilities with one another, knowing that they will be met with understanding and support. Partners in a trustworthy relationship provide mutual support, understanding, and valuable insights, making each other feel appreciated and valued.

Over time, a trusting relationship yields consistent benefits such as deeper emotional intimacy, greater relationship satisfaction, excellent resiliency against adversity, and a solid foundation for growth. These advantages underscore the importance of trust in a relationship. Stability in love is not a mystery. It comes from shared values, mutual support, and trust. Reflecting on what contributes to this stability can reassure you and reinforce these pillars in your relationship, making you feel more secure.

4 Dynamic Steps to Cultivate a Trusting Relationship

Building a strong foundation of trust in any relationship is not just important; it's crucial for its growth and longevity. Here's a vibrant action plan to guide you through the process, helping you stay committed and dedicated.

Step 1: Discover What Makes the Relationship Secure – Use the reflective questions below to identify what contributes to feelings of security and lasting connection in your relationship. Please rate your answer from 1 to 5, with 1 being the least important and 5 being the most important. Each partner answers independently and then shares their responses. Score responses to prioritize elements that resonate most with each partner and identify areas for improvement.

What Makes Us Feel Secure in Our Relationship?

Do you feel more secure when your partner is only physically available?

Do you feel more secure when your partner is emotionally available?

Does consistent communication make you feel more valued?

How important is trust in decision-making for your sense of security?

Do you feel secure when your partner follows his commitments?

Does physical affection strengthen your connection?

How does conflict resolution affect your feelings of stability?

Do goals and plans for the future feel that the relationship is lasting?

Do regular check-ins about your needs contribute to a sense of security?

How important are shared routines or rituals for creating stability?

Do you feel more secure when your partner acknowledges your emotions?

Step 2: Guided Discussion with Questions – After identifying the key elements, engage in a guided conversation with these questions to explore and deepen understanding:

What do you think has been the most essential factor in our relationship?

What actions or behavior of mine make you feel most secure?

Do you define trust in our relationship, and how can we strengthen it?

What's one thing I could do more to make you feel valued and loved?

What do you think when we talk about our future together?

What excites or reassures you?

When was the last time you felt especially connected to me?

What contributed to that feeling?

What rituals do we have that make our relationship feel stable?

How can we improve how we handle disagreements?

What does emotional availability look like to you?

Are there any unmet needs or desires you want us to address together?

Step 3: Nurture Trust with Actionable Exercises – Once you've identified key elements, implement nurturing and strengthening strategies. Use these practical actions:

1. Schedule weekly or monthly check-ins. Use prompts like:

"What's going well?",
"What challenges are we facing?" or
"What can we work on together?"

2. Trust-Building Actions - Consistency is key! Show up for each other and follow through on promises to create a sense of security and dependable support. Please list your commitments and discuss how to uphold them. Examples include being on time, keeping promises, and honoring personal boundaries.

3. Reassurance Rituals. Acknowledge and cherish the little victories. Celebrating achievements not only strengthens your bond but also makes you feel more connected and appreciated within the relationship. Create rituals that reinforce security, such as Saying "I love you" before bed or when leaving the house. Also, write a weekly note of gratitude for your partner.

4. *Conflict Resolution Practice*: Use a structured method for resolving disagreements, such as active listening or the "pause and reflect" exercise. Focus on understanding rather than winning.

5. *Future Planning* – Set shared goals and discuss your dreams for the future, creating a sense of direction and teamwork. By Fostering an environment where both parties feel comfortable sharing thoughts and feelings, you empower each other. Active listening and honest dialogue can work wonders, boosting your confidence in the relationship.

Step 4: Create a Relationship Vision Board with symbols and words representing trust, love, and shared aspirations. Position it in a visible place as a reminder of your commitment. Trust builds over time, so prioritize emotional safety, communication, and respect. Together, you can foster a thriving relationship in love and trust.

Following these steps, you can build and nurture a trusting relationship that thrives on understanding and connection! Regular relationship check-ins empower partners to openly discuss their emotional needs, proactively resolve issues before they become significant problems, celebrate family milestones and achievements, and reinforce their commitment to one another. By prioritizing this, couples can foster a deeper connection and build a healthier, more resilient relationship.

Chapter Twelve

Don't Push My Buttons!

W hether you're dating in your first few months or have been dating for years, you must speak up and know what your partner wants. In this chapter, you will be taught how to express yourself in relationships and apply what you learn to your relationships. Communication is the bedrock of successful relationships, a bridge that connects love and partnership. The ability to express thoughts, feelings, and aspirations clearly and truly understand your partner's perspective is invaluable. This chapter is dedicated to active listening, a cornerstone of effective communication that has the potential to transform your relationship.

Critical Components of Active Listening

Active listening is not just a tool, it's a key to fostering emotional security. When partners listen carefully to each other, they validate each other's feelings, show empathy and understanding, and overcome challenges. This understanding can enlighten and empower you in your relationship.

Active listening is not just listening but also connecting fully with what your partner says and feels. In an increasingly busy world, achieving this ability can mean distinguishing between a hurried chat and an enlightened conversation. Learning to listen actively establishes a trusting, empathic, and mutually supportive relationship.

Put Active Listening into Your Relationship

Give your partner all the attention they need. Put your devices away, look at one another, and imply that you are there. For instance, if your partner says, *'I had a tough day at work,'* you could respond, *'It sounds like you had a challenging day at the office.'* This is a way of clarifying and demonstrating your involvement. When your partner has finished speaking, note what you have heard to gain a correct understanding.

Consider things from your spouse's point of view. This builds empathy and your partner's appreciation. Don't ignore body language and vocalizing. They often express just as much as words do. Deepen the discussion by asking questions that cannot be answered "yes" or "no." Embrace your partner's emotions even if you disagree.

By practicing effective communication, especially active listening, you will achieve reduced conflicts and open, transparent communication. Feeling heard and understood is a powerful catalyst for relationship satisfaction.

Despite our best efforts, there are barriers to active listening. Be mindful of what's happening in your conversation. Never interrupt or prepare your responses before your partner speaks. Controlling one's emotional responses is a key skill for maintaining objectivity and control in communication.

To build a fulfilling relationship, you must identify and assert your relationship needs. Self-awareness is the foundation of effective communication with your partner. Take the time to reflect on what is non-negotiable for you, both emotionally and functionally, within the relationship.

Determine whether you need emotional support, quality time, physical affection, shared goals and values, or a sense of personal space and independence. Once you clarify your desires, it becomes essential to express them confidently to your partner. Strong communication skills are not optional—they are a necessity.

Your goal is to convey your thoughts clearly while avoiding defensiveness or escalation into conflict. Effective communication is vital for nurturing and sustaining a thriving relationship. Identify your needs, express them assertively, minimize distractions, and engage in open dialogue. This approach will help you forge a more rewarding partnership.

Schedule dedicated time for discussions in an environment free of judgment, ensuring both partners feel empowered to share. Make ongoing communication a priority. If you encounter persistent challenges, seek professional guidance without hesitation. Remember, effective communication is a process that demands time, practice, and collaboration. The commitment you make will lead to more satisfying relationship.

Two Powerful Exercises to Sharpen Your Skills

Effectively mastering communication is crucial in both personal and professional environments. Here are two assertive exercises that will elevate your skills and ensure you excel

Exercise 1- "What I Heard vs. What I Meant"

By addressing misunderstandings with the "What I Heard vs. What I Meant" framework, couples can turn potential conflicts into opportunities for greater intimacy and understanding. It fosters mutual respect and ensures that both partners feel valued and heard. It encourages couples to distinguish between intent and perception, minimizing defensiveness while fostering empathy. By closing the gap between what was expressed, what was intended, and what was interpreted, this approach ensures that both partners feel acknowledged and valued.

When to Use: Identify a moment of miscommunication. During or after an argument where one or both partners feel misunderstood or if a comment triggers hurt or confusion.

Partner A says, *"Why didn't you text me earlier?"*

Partner B hears: *"You don't care enough about me to check in."*

What Partner A meant: *"I missed you and wanted to hear from you."*

Create a Safe Space and set the Intention: Agree to approach the exercise with curiosity and kindness, not blame. **Example:** *"I think there's been a misunderstanding. Can we clarify what we each meant?"*

Pause for Calm: If emotions are high, take a few minutes to calm down. When you are ready, begin the exercise:

Step 1: State What You Heard:

Partner A shares their perception of what they heard. For example: *"When you said, 'Why didn't you text me earlier?' I heard you were upset and felt I didn't care enough."*

Step 2: State What You Meant:

Partner B explains their true intent. Example: *"I meant that I missed you and hoped to hear from you earlier."*

Step 3: Summarize and Validate:

Partner A summarizes what they've learned. For example, *"So, you weren't upset—you just missed me and wanted to connect sooner."*

Partner B confirms or adjusts. For example, *"Yes, exactly. I wasn't upset; I just wanted to feel closer to you."*

Step 4: Switch Roles. If necessary, repeat the process with the other partner's perspective. Each partner takes turns being the speaker and listener, focusing on clarity and understanding.

Step 5: Resolve and Reconnect.

Acknowledge the Misunderstanding. For example, *"I understand now. I'm sorry I misunderstood your intention."*

Reaffirm Your Care for Each Other. For example, *"Thank you for explaining. I'll try to express myself more clearly next time."*

Real-Life Applications: "What I Heard vs. What I Meant" in Action

Partner A says: *"You've been spending so much time at work lately."*

Partner B hears: *"You don't care about me or our relationship."*

Partner A meant: *"I miss you and wish we could spend more time together."*

Using the Exercise:

Partner B: *"When you said that, I felt you accused me of not prioritizing our relationship."*

Partner A: *"I meant that I miss you and enjoy spending time together. I wasn't blaming you—I just feel a little lonely."*

Partner B: *"Oh, so you weren't criticizing me—just letting me know you'd like more time with me?"*

Partner A: *"Exactly. I really value our time together."*

Resolution: Both partners leave the conversation feeling understood rather than attacked or dismissed.

Key Principles for Success

Use "I" Statements: Focus on how you felt or interpreted something rather than accusing or blaming. For example, always use: *"I heard..."* instead of *"You said..."*

Be Open to Correction: Accept that your perception may not align with your partner's intent.

Stay Calm: Avoid interrupting or getting defensive. Let each person share.

Ask Clarifying Questions: If something isn't clear, gently ask for more explanation.

When one partner feels defensive or attacked, remember that redirecting the conversation toward the shared goal of clarity and understanding can lead to a more positive outcome. Use the assertive statement, *"We're on the same team—I want to understand your perspective."* This approach can foster a sense of hope and optimism in your relationship.

If one partner struggles to articulate their feelings, taking a step back before engaging in dialogue is crucial. Encourage each other to write down thoughts. This simple act can be a powerful tool in clarifying feelings and promoting effective communication. When conversations stray into unrelated issues, it's important to refocus by addressing one misunderstanding at a time. This approach helps to maintain focus and clarity, and ensures that each issue is given the attention it deserves. Set aside other topics for later discussion.

Exercise 2 - The "Pause and Reflect"

This is a structured approach to defusing conflict, fostering understanding, and maintaining intimacy during disagreements. It helps partners step away from reactive emotions, reflect on their feelings, and re-engage in a calmer, more constructive manner.

Objective: To interrupt heated arguments, create space for individual reflection, and facilitate respectful communication for resolving conflicts with love and understanding.

If voices are raised, emotions escalate, or the argument feels unproductive or hurtful, either partner can suggest a pause by saying something like, *"I think we're not really hearing each other right now. Can we pause and come back to this?"* or *"I need a moment to gather my thoughts so we can talk calmly."* Both partners commit to respecting the pause as a tool to reconnect rather than avoid the issue.

Separate Temporarily: Go to different rooms or sit quietly apart to allow both partners to reflect without immediate pressure.

Write Down Your Thoughts: Use pen and paper or a notes app to capture your feelings. Answer these prompts:

What am I feeling right now?
What triggered this feeling?
What is my underlying need or concern in this situation?
What outcome do I want for this conversation?
What can I take responsibility for in this conflict?

Engage in calming activities like deep breathing, a short walk, or listening to soothing music. These activities help reduce reactive emotions and create a space for clarity. After both partners have written down their feelings, exchange your notes or take turns reading them aloud. Focus on understanding, not rebutting, what your partner has expressed. As your partner shares, avoid interrupting or forming counterarguments in your mind. Instead, focus on genuinely hearing their perspective.

Return to the discussion to solve the issue together rather than "winning" the argument. Use "I" statements to express your feelings and needs clearly (e.g., *"I feel hurt when..."* instead of *"You always..."*). Ask clarifying questions, such as: *"Can you help me understand what you mean by that?"* or "How can I make you feel heard in this situation?". Brainstorm solutions together. Please ensure that both partners feel their concerns are addressed. For example, *"Let's set aside time every weekend to plan our schedules so we avoid misunderstandings."*

End the conversation with a positive affirmation of your relationship, such as *"I love you and want us to work through this together"* or *"Thank you for helping me understand your feelings."* Hug each other, hold hands, or express gratitude for calmly resolving the conflict.

The "Pause and Reflect" in Action

Scenario: Partner A feels overwhelmed with household responsibilities, while Partner B feels unappreciated for their contributions.

During the argument, Partner A says, *"I need a moment to reflect so we can approach this calmly."*

Partner A writes: *"I feel stressed because I feel like I'm doing most of the housework. I need support and acknowledgment."*

Partner B writes: *"I feel unappreciated because I try to help in other ways, but it seems like it's not enough."*

Partner A reads their reflection, and Partner B listens. Then, Partner B shares their perspective. They agree to create a shared chore list and regularly thank each other for their contributions. They hugged and expressed gratitude for resolving the issue together.

When one partner resists taking a pause due to fear of avoidance, it is crucial to establish a specific time to resume the conversation. For instance, assertively state, *"We need to take 20 minutes and reconvene at 6:30."*

If one partner tends to stew or ruminate, direct your reflections toward actionable insights instead of assigning blame. Remember, you both share a mutual objective-to resolve the issue with love and understanding. This unity of purpose can help you stay focused and avoid unnecessary conflicts.

If conversations derail after the pause, take charge by referencing your written reflections and remember to tackle one issue at a time. This approach can help you stay focused and avoid feeling overwhelmed by multiple issues at once.

Why This Exercise Works:

Allowing time for reflection is crucial in preventing arguments from escalating into hurtful exchanges. Writing down our emotions is an effective way to gain clarity and identify underlying needs. When we share our reflections, it fosters empathy and reduces defensiveness. Ending discussions with a gesture of reconnection is essential; it reinforces that love is the foundation of our relationship, even in the midst of disagreements.

By practicing the "Pause and Reflect" Exercise, couples can transform conflicts into opportunities for growth, understanding, and deeper intimacy.

Mastering communication, particularly active listening, takes patience and practice. By spending time and energy learning to talk better with your partner, you build a foundation for a happier, more patient, and stable relationship. If you work on these abilities, your relationship will be more powerful, satisfying, and enduring than ever.

Chapter Thirteen

The Power of "I" Statements

L earning to say 'I' sentences can transform any relationship, turning the complicated communication dance into a harmonious rhythm. This powerful method not only clarifies but also fosters empathy between partners. Let's delve into how these five simple statements can revolutionize your relationship and pave the way for deeper connections.

At its core, an 'I' statement is a straightforward form of communication. It's not about assigning blame but about sharing your experience. It brings your feelings and opinions to the forefront, making your words safe for open dialogue.

So, for example, rather than *"You never listen to me,"* you might say, *"I don't feel heard when we talk"*. This simple change can mean the difference between a successful conversation and a failure.

Mastering 'I' statements is not just a skill—it's essential for effective relationship communication. To assertively convey your feelings and foster understanding, follow these key components:

1. Identify Your Feelings: Clearly pin down your emotions. Acknowledge if you are tired, frustrated, or content—be specific about what you're experiencing.

2. Describe the Situation: This is your opportunity to Paint a clear picture of the context. Provide precise details about the event or circumstance triggering your feelings. The more you can help the other person understand the situation, the more connected you'll feel.

3. Explain the Impact: Articulate how this situation affects you personally and underscore the importance of addressing it.

4. Propose a Solution: 'I' statements also play a crucial role in proposing a solution. By Presenting a constructive action or change that would help improve the situation, you take the initiative in seeking a resolution. This is where the power of 'I' statements truly shines.

For instance: *"When the housework gets to be too much (sentence), I feel overwhelmed (feeling). It makes me nervous about how we will continue (effect). Can we develop a chore schedule together (answer)?"*

'I' statements are essential tools in effective communication. By focusing on personal experiences rather than making accusations, they significantly reduce the chances of defensive reactions from partners. This creates an open and safe environment for discussion. 'I' statements are crucial for deepening understanding between partners, as they illuminate feelings and needs clearly.

When partners identify their emotions and needs upfront, they can swiftly collaborate on finding solutions. Utilizing 'I' statements consistently ensures both partners remain attuned to each other's feelings, strengthening the relationship.

Real-Life Applications

Take these 'I' statements and think about how they can change mundane relationship situations:

Instead of saying, *"You're always on your phone,"* try: *"I feel cut off when we're together, and phones are working. Do we need some screen time?"*

Instead of: *"You never babysit."* Try: *"I have trouble keeping children on my own. I wish we could distribute these duties more evenly".*

List of additional 'I' statements for different occasions

Acknowledging Feelings: *"I can see this is important to you."*

Expressing Understanding: *"I understand how you feel; it's completely valid."*

Inviting Dialogue: *"I'd love to hear more about your perspective."*

Offering Support: *"How can I support you through this?"*

Validating Concerns: *"It makes sense that you feel this way, given the circumstances."*

Encouraging Openness: *"I appreciate you sharing this with me; it takes courage."*

Reflecting Emotions: *"It sounds like you're feeling [insert emotion], is that right?"*

Clarifying Intentions: *"I intend to understand you better; can we explore this together?"*

Expressing Gratitude: *"Thank you for trusting me with your feelings."*

Acknowledging Differences: *"I respect that we may see this differently; let's talk about it."*

Taking a Pause: *"Can we take a moment to breathe and gather our thoughts?"*

Expressing Calmness: *"I want to approach this calmly because I care about our relationship."*

Acknowledging Emotions: *"I can sense that we're both feeling really strongly right now."*

Finding Common Ground: *"We both want what's best; let's find a solution together."*

Using "I" Statements: *"I feel upset when this happens; it makes me feel [insert emotion]."*

Requesting Clarification: *"Can you help me understand your point of view better?"*

Offering to Listen: *"I'm here to listen to your concerns; please share your feelings."*

Apologizing if Necessary: *"I'm sorry if my words hurt you; that wasn't my intention."*

In a relationship, saying "I" multiple times builds trust, warmth, and respect from your partner. This makes the conversation free and open, leading to closer understanding and connection.

Chapter Fourteen

Navigate Tough Talks

C ommunication is key if you want a successful relationship. Whether your issues are old or new, how you deal with them will significantly affect your relationship. With the right attitude and practice, you can turn adversity into a golden opportunity for self- and relationship development. Before taking difficult discussions, ensure you're putting in place a good vibe for the conversations. This empowering strategy opens up the possibility for healthy communication that will build your relationship. Here are some fundamental things to keep in mind:

Select the Right Time and Place: Sit quietly in a quiet environment. Ensure that both partners are relaxed.

Adopt a Constructive Mindset: Take the discussion seriously. Focus on strengthening the relationship, not winning an argument.

Clarify Your Goals: Describe what you want to gain from the discussion. Keep the conversation about solving problems and improving your relationship at the forefront. Once you've done this, use these strategies to help increase understanding and create a welcoming environment:

Stay on Topic: Avoid unrelated areas that could increase tension. Remain focused on the issue at hand.

Use "I" Statements: Share your thoughts and experiences without blaming anyone. (For instance: "I feel bad when..." rather than "You always...")

Ask Open-Ended Questions: Allow your partner to open up about what's happening in their head. For example, "What do you think of...?" instead of "Why did you...?"

Practice Active Listening: Listen as intently as possible to what your partner is saying. Then, review the words you've heard to ensure you understand them.

Managing Emotions During Challenging Discussions

When facing difficult conversations, it's crucial to remain calm and composed. Here are effective strategies to help you stay relaxed and focused:

Deep Breathing Exercises: Embrace the power of slow, deep breaths to center yourself and calm your nervous system. These exercises, when practiced regularly, can significantly reduce the intensity of your emotions, making you more composed and in control during difficult conversations.

Mindfulness Practices: Remember, it's not just about the conversation, but also how you end it. If the discussion becomes overwhelming, take a brief break to gather your thoughts and regain your composure. Make it a point to conclude difficult discussions on a positive note. This positive ending can significantly influence the overall outcome of the conversation.

Acknowledge the progress you've made and appreciate the efforts both partners have invested. Shift your focus to the positive aspects of your relationship. Remember, each challenging discussion is a valuable opportunity to deepen your connection with your partner. Prioritizing these conversations will foster more satisfying and stable relationships.

I truly appreciate you grabbing a
copy of my book!
Just scan this QR code to access your
exciting interactive workbook!

The "Love Reset Ritual" is a meaningful way to close conflicts and restore emotional and physical connection between partners. It helps shift the focus from disagreement to mutual appreciation, reinforcing the foundation of love and trust.

Transform Conflict into Connection with the "Love Reset Ritual" (as outlined in the Workbook). Make sure to download and utilize the attached interactive workbook to achieve the best results possible! Your success is just a click away!

Love Reset Ritual

Objective: To reconnect emotionally and rebuild intimacy after resolving a conflict, ensuring that both partners feel heard, valued, and reassured about the strength of their bond.

Detailed Instructions: Set the Tone for Reconnection.

Choose a Calm Moment: Once the conflict has been resolved or emotions have settled, agree to engage in a Love Reset Ritual. Example: *"I think we've reached a good understanding. Let's do our reset ritual to move forward together."*

Create a Safe Space: Sit or stand facing each other in a private, quiet area. Optional: Light a candle, play calming music, or hold hands to set an optimistic and intimate tone.

Share Three Positive Things About Each Other: Each partner shares three positive things about the other. These can relate to the conflict or general qualities you love and admire. Examples:

"I appreciate your patience while we talked through this."
"I love how much effort you put into understanding my feelings."
"You always find a way to make me smile, even when things are tough."

Sharing positives shifts focus away from the conflict and reinforces mutual appreciation.

Choose a Meaningful Gesture: Hold hands, hug, or touch each other's hearts to re-establish physical closeness. For a more profound connection, synchronize your breathing by taking slow, deep breaths together for a minute. Physical touch fosters the release of oxytocin, helping to calm nerves and build trust after emotional strain.

Express Commitment: Affirm your love and commitment to moving forward positively. Examples: *"I love you and am committed to working through challenges with you."* or *"I'm grateful we can discuss our differences and become stronger."*

Offer Apologies if Needed: If you feel hurt lingering, briefly acknowledge them with sincere apologies. For example, "I'm sorry for the way I reacted earlier. I'll work on being more mindful next time."

Create a Symbolic Gesture to Mark the Reset as:

1 .Lighting a Candle: Symbolize a fresh start by lighting a candle together.

2. Sharing a Toast: Pour a cup of tea, wine, or sparkling water, and toast to your love.

3. Writing It Down: Jot down a short statement like "We're moving forward with love" and keep it as a reminder.

End with a Shared Moment of Joy: To lighten the mood and re-establish playfulness, watch a funny video, share a memory, or make a silly joke. Example: "Remember when we argued over who loved pizza more?"

Example of a Love Reset Ritual

Set the Scene: Sit facing each other on the couch, holding hands.

Share Positives: Partner A: "I love how open you were about your feelings. I admire your honesty."Partner B: "I appreciate how you stayed calm and focused on finding a solution."

Physical Reconnection: Share a long hug, syncing your breathing.

Affirm Commitment: Partner A: *"I'm so glad we worked through this. I love you and want us to keep growing together."* Partner B: *"Me too. I'm committed to making sure we feel supported and loved."*

Symbolic Gesture: Light a candle and say, *"Here's to a fresh start."*

Tips for Success

Be Genuine: Speak from the heart when sharing positives or affirmations.

Keep It Simple: Avoid overcomplicating the ritual—it's about connection, not perfection.

Make It a Habit: Use the Love Reset Ritual consistently to build a pattern of healthy conflict resolution.

Why the Love Reset Ritual Works?

The Love Reset Ritual is a powerful tool that reinforces positivity by directing focus toward appreciation, effectively dissolving lingering tension. It firmly reassures both partners that love is the unwavering foundation of their relationship, even amidst disagreements. This ritual enhances intimacy through purposeful physical touch, and affirmations serve to strengthen both emotional and physical connections. By consistently practicing reconnection after conflicts, couples can decisively transform challenges into valuable opportunities for growth.

Chapter Fifteen

Tackle Sensitive Issues

Often, couples in relationships face uncomfortable discussions. Yet, these challenging conversations can be life-altering, enabling both partners to develop and achieve clarity. This chapter covers how to transform potentially contentious conversational exchanges into opportunities for bonding. There is nothing inherently wrong about relationships that engender conflict. Debates can be highly productive personally and in relationships if you frame them with the right mindset. By seeing uncomfortable conversations as opportunities to grow and develop, couples can find more understanding of one another's views, uncover underlying needs and desires, and develop vital problem-solving skills together.

To make difficult conversations more manageable, you must:

1. Identify Root Causes: Look beyond surface-level disagreements to understand the underlying issues or needs. This is crucial for comprehending the genuine reasons behind the conflict.

2. *Collaborate on Solutions:* Brainstorm ideas and strive to find solutions that benefit both parties. This approach fosters a collaborative and respectful environment.

3. *Engage in Active Listening:* This practice shows respect for your partner's perspective. Focus your full attention on your partner and aim to understand their viewpoint before expressing your own.

4. *Use "I" Statements:* Share your thoughts without sounding accusatory. For example, say, "I get angry when..." instead of "You always...".

These techniques can help create a more constructive dialogue.

Creating an Environment for Difficult Conversations

Establishing a strong foundation for difficult conversations is paramount. To do this effectively, choose a time when both partners are calm and ready to engage. This strategic approach not only empowers both partners but also reassures them, fostering a more productive and confident dialogue. Agree to take breaks if emotions start to rise, knowing that this is a sign of respect for each other's feelings.

Maintain respect at all times by avoiding name-calling and personal insults. Focus squarely on the issue at hand, not on each other. This commitment is not just essential, it's a cornerstone in creating a secure environment that is critical for a healthy relationship. It's a way of showing each other that you value and respect their feelings and opinions.

Understanding your partner's perspective and expressing empathy, even if you disagree, is vital. This not only deepens your connection but also reinforces mutual respect. It's a way of showing that you care and are willing to understand their point of view. Actively seek solutions that fulfill the needs of both partners. Aligning individual and relational priorities is crucial for maintaining harmony.

Mastering the dynamics of giving and receiving is key to lasting relationships. Remember, compromise does not mean sacrificing your values; it's about finding solutions that benefit both parties. After a challenging discussion, take the necessary time to reflect on the process. Evaluate what worked and identify areas for improvement. Acknowledge each other's contributions to the resolution and pinpoint strategies to enhance future discussions, such as active listening, setting clear boundaries, and practicing patience.

The "Pause, Clarify, and Connect" Framework

This structured exercise blends emotional regulation with empathetic listening, offering a step-by-step approach to handling sensitive conversations gracefully.

Step 1: Pause to ground yourself
Take three deep breaths together: This helps calm the nervous system.
Acknowledge emotions silently: Identify your feelings (e.g., hurt, frustration, fear) without assigning blame.
Decide on timing: If either partner feels too overwhelmed, agree to revisit the conversation after a brief break.

Step 2: Ask clarifying questions to create mutual understanding

"Can you help me understand what's most important to you here?"
"What do you need from me to feel safe sharing this?"

Restate what you hear: Partner A: *"I'm hearing that you feel ___ because ___. Is that right?"*

Partner B: Confirm or clarify.

Step 3: Avoid assumptions: If something isn't clear, ask, "Can you explain what you mean by that?"

Step 4: Connect to repair and rebuild trust. Express appreciation:

"Thank you for being honest about this. I know it's not easy."
"I appreciate you trusting me with your feelings."

And collaborate on a solution:

"What's one small step we can take together to improve this?"
"How can we ensure we both feel good about moving forward?"

End with a positive note: Share a hope or goal for your relationship moving forward. For example: *"I hope we can continue being honest like this—it brings us closer."*

Practice Reflective Questions

These sample questions will help couples explore their emotions, intentions, and needs without being defensive:

"What did I say or do in this conversation that made you feel unheard?"

"Is there a part of this issue that feels especially hard to discuss? Can you help me understand why?"

"What do you think I'm misunderstanding about your perspective?"

"If you could wave a magic wand, what would the resolution to this look like for you?"

"What's one thing I could do right now to make you feel more supported?"

"Is there a way we can approach this differently to make it feel less tense for both of us?"

"What's an example of a time we handled a tough conversation well? Can we try to replicate that?"

"What do you think we both might be afraid of in this situation?"

"What's one thing you're grateful for about me, even during this disagreement?"

"If we focus on the bigger picture, what's the most important thing for us to remember right now?"

This reflection exercise builds positive conflict-management habits and helps you get ready for what comes next.

Couples can learn from difficult conversations and use the dialogue to improve relationships by bringing it into openness, respect, and learning. As you know, the aim is not to avoid conflict but to deal with it in a way that will strengthen your connection. With practice and patience, you can use even the most difficult conversations as scaffolding for a stronger, more open relationship.

Chapter Sixteen

The Significance of Quality Time

B uilding a strong relationship takes more than just sharing time; it's about maximizing each moment with purposeful, meaningful inter-actions. This chapter highlights the significance of quality time together and how it can transform your relationship by creating impactful experiences and deeper connections.

Quality time serves as the cornerstone of a fulfilling relationship. It isn't measured by the hours spent together but by the depth of our connection during those times. Couples can foster open conversations and nurture emotional bonds by prioritizing authentic presence over simple proximity, ultimately enriching their relationship.

Best Ways to Foster Deeper Connections

Active listening, which includes techniques like paraphrasing, reflecting, and clarifying, is a powerful tool for relationship growth. When you give your partner your full attention in conversations, you hear their words and understand their emotions and thoughts. This level of engagement can foster a deeper connection and mutual understanding.

Sharing vulnerabilities is not a sign of weakness, but a key to building trust and intimacy in a relationship. When you speak honestly about your fears, desires, and dreams, you create a safe space for both partners to express themselves without fear of judgment. This openness can strengthen your bond and deepen your connection, making you feel more secure in your relationship.

Exploring new topics is not just a way to keep your conversations fresh and engaging, but a path to growth in your relationship. Whether you and your partner discuss a book you both read, debate the news, or ponder philosophical issues, these discussions can spark new ideas and perspectives, keeping your relationship dynamic and exciting.

To make the most of your time together:

1. Schedule regular evenings when all distractions are off. Use this time for meaningful conversations or activities that help you feel connected.

2. Plan weekly or biweekly date nights. These don't have to be extravagant; even a simple dinner at home can be special if you focus on each other.

3. Start your day with a few minutes of personal space and a cup of coffee.

4. Connect with one another before the day's demands begin.

Navigating the Demands of Our Busy Lives

In our fast-paced world, time is a valuable resource. Prioritizing your relationship just as you would any vital work obligation is crucial. Make the most of small time slots and seize every opportunity for meaningful conversations. Even brief moments, such as during a car ride or while preparing dinner, can lead to impactful discussions.

Pursue shared interests by engaging in activities that you both love. Commit to exploring new hobbies together, enrolling in classes, or organizing regular outings that you both enjoy. Focus on building solid interactions that strengthen your emotional connection. These discussions provide valuable insights into each other's values, help you address challenges, encourage shared dreams, establish clear goals, and allow you to express appreciation and gratitude.

By implementing these strategies, you can enhance your relationship amidst the demands of a busy life, ensuring that it thrives and grows stronger.

27 Questions to Inspire Meaningful Conversations

What's one belief or value that has shaped who you are today?

What makes you feel happiest in our relationship?

What from your childhood still influences the way you approach life?

How do you see your values aligning with or differing from mine?

What's a decision or life lesson you're most proud of, and why?

What is the most essential quality in a healthy relationship, and why?

How do you like to give and receive love differently?

What would your life look like if we hadn't met?

What challenges have we handled well, and what made it work?

How could we improve the way we handle disagreements?

What's a current stressor in your life that I can help alleviate?

How can we better balance our personal and shared needs?

How can I better support you when you're feeling overwhelmed or upset?

How effectively do we manage our responsibilities?

What could we work on together to strengthen our relationship?

What's a new skill or hobby you'd like us to learn or explore together?

What would it look like if you could design the perfect day for us next year?

What's one place in the world you'd love to visit with me, and why?

What's a shared goal we haven't discussed yet that you'd like us to pursue?

How do you envision our relationship evolving as we grow older?

What have I done recently that made you feel loved and supported?

How have I changed or improved your life since we've been together?

What's one quality you admire most about me, and why?

What everyday gesture do I do that you appreciate but do not mention?

How do you feel I've helped you grow as a person?

What's our memory that makes you smile whenever you think about it?

How do we bring out the best in each other?

These questions are crucial for cultivating vulnerability and deep emotional intimacy. They demand that you reflect on shared values and aspirations, foster gratitude, and thereby strengthen the connection between partners. You will build a relationship that lasts and thrives by dedicating time to each other and engaging in meaningful, genuine communication. Remember, the essence of a strong relationship lies not in the quantity of time spent together but in the quality of that time. Living mindfully and communicating thoughtfully in the present moment, you will create a dynamic, life-sustaining partnership with your significant other.

Chapter Seventeen

Pillow Talk: Discussing Intimacy

Maintaining a passionate state in relationships is essential, yet it's a challenge that many couples face. Over time, lovers often become too comfortable, allowing the initial spark to fade. This chapter emphasizes the necessity of revitalizing your sex life through open conversation and spontaneity.

Engaging in pillow talk is a powerful way to deepen intimacy in relationships. It creates a safe space for open dialogue about feelings, desires, and vulnerabilities, strengthening the emotional connection between partners. Embrace these moments to explore each other's thoughts and dreams, making your bond even more fulfilling. Don't underestimate the value of these intimate conversations — they pave the way for a more meaningful relationship.

It's crucial to recognize that many couples drift into disinterest without realizing it. Scheduled meetings, predictable sex, and monotonous routines dull the vibrancy of intimacy. While routine provides structure, it can also stifle passion, reducing passionate encounters to mere tasks. If you're determined to break free from this cycle, consider these assertive strategies:

Discover Exciting New Spaces: Don't confine your intimacy to the bedroom. Take advantage of your home's hidden gems or seek secluded outdoor locations for intimate moments. Transform overlooked areas into romantic settings to inject freshness and excitement into your relationship.

Play with Timing: Don't wait for the "right" time; create thrilling moments of intimacy whenever possible. Embrace the exhilaration of morning passion and the allure of evening romantic endeavors, and surprise your partner with spontaneous kisses during the day. Mixing up the timing will shatter the monotony and keep the excitement alive.

Inject excitement: Embrace the unexpected to reignite the flames of passion. Organize surprise picnics, spontaneous weekend getaways, or playful date nights – these can refresh your love life. Send heartfelt love notes and create delightful surprises to keep the spark thriving.

90 Romantic and Sex "Would You Rather" Questions

Would you rather receive a love letter or a surprise romantic gift?

Would you rather have a candlelit dinner at home or at a fancy restaurant?

Would you rather slow dance under the stars or snuggle by a cozy fire?

Would you rather be surprised with flowers or a hidden love note?

Would you rather take a spontaneous weekend getaway or have a carefully planned vacation?

Would you rather watch the sunrise together or the sunset?

Would you choose to celebrate our anniversary through a grand gesture that creates lasting memories, or would you rather savor a peaceful moment together, enjoying each other's company?

Would you rather share a couple's spa day or go on an adventurous date?

Would you prefer to be serenaded with a song or lost in a slow dance?

Would you rather have a partner who surprises you often or one who creates meaningful traditions?

Would you rather spend a rainy day cuddled up or dancing in the rain?

Would you rather create a scrapbook of your memories or write a journal?

Would you rather celebrate Valentine's Day with a lavish outing or an intimate evening at home?

Would you rather have a picnic in a secluded park or at a rooftop restaurant?

Would you rather exchange small, meaningful gifts or share an experience?

Would you rather write each other love poems or share a playlist of songs?

Would you rather walk on the beach together or hike to a scenic overlook?

Would you rather stargaze on a clear night or watch a fireworks together?

Would you rather cook a romantic meal together or be surprised with breakfast in bed?

Would you rather hear "I love you" daily or feel it through acts of kindness?

Would you rather receive a surprise visit at work or a romantic text?

Would you rather spend a lazy Sunday morning together or an adventurous Saturday afternoon?

Would you rather share a dance at a wedding or create your private dance at home?

Would you rather exchange glances across a crowded room or share a quiet moment holding hands in public?

Would you rather revisit where you had your first date or explore somewhere new?

Would you rather ride on a Ferris wheel together or a romantic boat ride?

Would you rather have a partner who surprises you with romantic gestures or one who plans significant ones?

Would you rather write a love story about your relationship or create a photo album capturing its highlights?

Would you rather spend an evening sharing your dreams for the future or reflecting on your favorite memories together?

Would you rather fall asleep holding hands or wake up to a morning kiss?

Would you rather try a new position every week or stick to favorite?

Would you rather make love in a romantic setting like a beach or a daring location like an elevator?

Would you rather focus on long, slow intimacy or short, intense sessions?

Would you rather have a massage turn into lovemaking or start with passionate kissing?

Would you rather experiment with temperature play (e.g., ice cubes or warmth) or sensory deprivation (e.g., blindfolds)?

Would you rather explore role-playing together or try sex toys?

Would you rather be the initiator or let your partner take the lead?

Would you rather have sex in the morning or at night?

Would you rather experience passionate sex with music or complete silence?

Would you rather wholly focus on one partner's pleasure or balance both simultaneously?

Would you rather have a spontaneous encounter or plan a sexy evening?

Would you rather spend an hour exploring foreplay or go straight to the main act?

Would you rather make love under the stars or in front of a cozy fireplace?

Would you rather experiment with different outfits or focus on new physical techniques?

Would you rather kiss for hours or focus on full-body touch?

Would you rather keep the lights on to see each other or off to enhance the mystery?

Would you rather spend time teasing each other or jump right into passionate intimacy?

Would you rather explore aromatherapy during sex or experiment with food?

Would you rather prioritize endurance or playfulness in the bedroom?

Would you rather keep things lighthearted and fun or fiery and intense?

Would you rather have a full day of sensual build-up or one intense hour of passion?

Would you rather explore intimacy in water or on a luxurious bed?

Would you rather include playful teasing or serious, focused touch?

Would you rather try tantric breathing or wild, uninhibited passion?

Would you rather experiment with sensual dancing before sex or engage in playful chasing games?

Would you rather explore mutual self-touch or guided touch with each other?

Would you rather engage in intimacy that is slow and tender or fast and exhilarating?

Would you rather incorporate soft restraints like scarves or experiment with sensory overload (e.g., intense lighting or sounds)?

Would you rather prioritize spontaneity in different locations or consistent intimacy in a comfortable space?

Would you rather focus on building flexibility with yoga-inspired positions or strength for lifting and movement?

Would you rather feel deeply connected before sex or let intimacy build during the act?

Would you rather talk openly about your fantasies beforehand or let them come up naturally during lovemaking?

Would you rather prioritize your emotional or your physical bond?

Would you rather share how you feel after sex or reflect silently and cuddle?

Would you rather your partner expresses their love verbally or through actions during intimacy?

Would you rather experience a playful, light-hearted intimacy or a profoundly emotional and serious one?

Would you rather focus on building trust in your connection or spontaneity in your sex life?

Would you rather express vulnerability in bed or feel empowerment?

Would you rather have talks about desires or learn by exploring together?

Would you rather hear affirmations of your attractiveness during sex or see them through gestures?

Would you rather explore intimacy that strengthens your emotional bond or builds physical confidence?

Would you rather have a partner who shares their most profound feelings before sex or during pillow talk afterward?

Would you rather share your fears about intimacy openly or focus on the positive aspects?

Would you rather laugh and connect emotionally during intimacy or feel wholly swept away by passion?

Would you rather feel adored as a partner or respected as a lover?

Would you rather explore the meaning of your connection after sex or deepen it through physical affection?

Would you rather ask your partner about their emotional needs or share yours first?

Would you rather talk about the emotional significance of sex or let your actions show your connection?

Would you rather spend time journaling together about your intimacy or talk about it over dinner?

Would you rather create rituals around intimacy (like candles and meaningful words) or keep things spontaneous?

Would you rather have deep eye contact throughout intimacy or share loving words afterward?

Would you rather explore a partner's emotional vulnerabilities or share your own before lovemaking?

Would you rather prioritize emotional healing through sex or use it as a celebration of joy?

Would you rather hear affirmations of love before or during intimacy?

Would you rather cuddle in silence after sex or talk about it?

Would you rather explore the ways your childhood shaped your views on intimacy or focus on how your relationship has grown?

Would you rather talk about what sex means to you emotionally or physically before being intimate?

Would you rather build sexual tension through meaningful gestures or spontaneous acts of affection?

Would you rather make love as a way to resolve conflicts or as a way to celebrate your bond?

Would you rather be surprised by a partner's emotional openness or gently ease into deeper emotional conversations?

According to neuroscientist Stephanie Cacioppo, new experiences foster more profound love and bonding. Be proactive in cultivating cherished moments, and infuse your marriage with playfulness and spontaneity. Take charge and transform your relationship today!

Use the interactive workbook as a roadmap to clearly document your preferences. This powerful tool guides couples through the process, enabling them to outline their reflections and create a practical strategy for cultivating a vibrant, healthy relationship.

Chapter Eighteen

Reignite the Spark

Lasting love is firmly rooted in compatibility, trust, and experience. Communication and honesty are essential for couples who aim to sustain a long-term relationship. It's crucial to express our feelings, hopes, and fears openly, without fear of repercussions. Equally vital is spending quality time together, whether through new adventures or simply enjoying each other's company, as it helps in maintaining passion.

Consistent expression of gratitude, even for the smallest acts, significantly impacts the relationship. Learning to lean on each other during challenging times and celebrating successes brings deep satisfaction. A strong partnership thrives on teamwork, appreciation for each other's differences, and ongoing personal growth. Equally crucial is the ability to forgive, let go of minor irritations, and maintain a forward-looking perspective. By prioritizing these elements, couples cultivate enduring love that enriches their relationship for generations.

Love is dynamic, and prioritizing commitment ensures you remain connected through adversity. Supporting your partner during stressful periods solidifies trust and loyalty, even in complex situations. Partners in lasting relationships not only embrace change but actively grow together. Adapting to new roles, such as becoming parents or navigating career shifts, builds resilience. Healthy relationships honor individuality while fostering shared experiences, which bring joy and a sense of togetherness. This can include pursuing personal hobbies while making time for regular date nights.

Reflect on what qualities or dynamics in your relationship feel timeless. Identify ways to reinforce them, ensuring your love stands the test of time.

Long-Term Strategies for Relationship Growth

Investing in growth as a couple is essential for ensuring that your relationship remains dynamic, resilient, and fulfilling over time.

Align on mutual goals to work effectively toward a shared vision. Define clear objectives, such as saving for a house, planning a trip to a dream destination, or starting a family together.

Acknowledge both big and small achievements to reinforce positivity and connection in your relationship. Celebrate milestones and everyday successes through handwritten notes, special outings, or thoughtful gifts.

Prioritize undistracted moments to reconnect regularly. Schedule a weekly date night without fail, even during busy periods—this is non-negotiable for maintaining your bond.

Engage in learning together by attending workshops, reading relationship-oriented books, or listening to insightful podcasts. Dive into topics like love languages to deepen your understanding of each other's needs.

Reflection: Identify specific long-term goals or traditions you can establish to ensure your relationship continues to evolve positively.

Nurturing Love Through Thoughtful Communication

Communication is the heartbeat of lasting love. Thoughtful, intentional conversations help couples feel heard, valued, and supported.

Daily Affirmations: Express appreciation and love regularly. For example, "I love how you make me laugh even on hard days."

Deep Conversations: To maintain emotional intimacy, discuss dreams, fears, and aspirations. For example, "What's one goal you'd love to accomplish in the next five years?"

Conflict Resolution Skills: Respect disagreements and focus on solutions. For example, Saying, "I see your perspective, and I'd like to find a compromise," promotes collaboration over confrontation.

Playfulness: Humor and light-hearted banter keep the relationship fun and engaging. For example, They Text each other funny memes or share jokes during the day.

Reflection: How does your current communication style nurture or hinder your connection? What changes could deepen your bond?

Lets Play "The Question Game"

The Question Game is a fun and meaningful activity where couples take turns asking and answering questions to deepen their understanding of each other. It encourages vulnerability, curiosity, and connection.

Objective: To foster intimacy by learning more about your partner's thoughts, dreams, and feelings in a playful yet thoughtful way.

Set the Scene: Choose a quiet, comfortable space to focus on each other without distractions. Light candles, play soft music or pour a drink to make the environment more romantic.

Prepare the Questions: Utilize the interactive workbook provided to determine your preference for working on paper or screen. Use the questions below or develop your own. Make sure to incorporate a mix of serious, thoughtful questions along with some light-hearted or playful ones.

Take Turns Asking and Answering: One partner asks a question and the other answers. Then, switch roles. Encourage honesty and active listening. Avoid interrupting or judging.

Dig Deeper: If an answer sparks curiosity, ask follow-up questions to explore further. Example: *"Why is that memory so meaningful to you?"* or *"What inspired that dream?"*

Play Until Satisfied: Set a timer (e.g., 20–30 minutes) or keep playing until you feel connected.

30 Questions for the Game

What's a dream you've never shared with me?

What would it be if you could relive one moment in our relationship?

What's a quirky habit of mine that you secretly love?

What's one thing about our relationship that makes you proud?

If you could describe me in three words, what would they be?

What's a silly memory of us that always makes you laugh?

If money weren't an issue, what would be your ideal date with me?

What's something small I do that makes your day better?

Where we will go if we could travel anywhere in the world together?

What's one thing you admire about me that I may not know?

How do you feel most supported by me?

What's one of your happiest childhood memories?

If you could learn a new skill, what would it be and why?

What's a fear or insecurity you've never shared with anyone else?

What's the best gift I've ever given you and why?

How do you feel when I [specific action, like "hold your hand"]?

What's one thing you'd like us to do together more often?

What's a quality of mine that you hope never changes?

If you could live in any era or period, which would it be and why?

What's one way I can make you feel more loved?

What's your favorite compliment I've ever given you?

What's one adventure you'd love to go on together?

If you could switch lives with anyone, who would it be and why?

What's your favorite thing about how we resolve disagreements?

What romantic gesture would you love for me to do for you?

What's a habit or routine you have that you cherish?

What specific moment made you realize how deeply you love me?

If you write a letter to your future self, what love advice would you give?

What's one thing you want us to try or experiment?

How do you envision our relationship growing in the next 5 years?

It's essential to align on shared goals and create a clear roadmap for your future together. This process will not only bring you closer but will also solidify your commitment to one another. Take the time to discuss where you envision your relationship in five, ten, and twenty years. Write down your shared visions, including career aspirations, family goals, and lifestyle preferences. Then, create a detailed plan that includes actionable steps toward these objectives. Discuss how envisioning your future together not only brings clarity but also ignites excitement in your relationship.

Celebrating your journey together is equally important. Reflect on key moments and set ambitious new milestones. Acknowledge the progress you've made, and use it as motivation for what lies ahead. Develop a timeline of significant relationship milestones, such as your first date, the first "I love you," and moving in together. Identify upcoming milestones that you'd like to achieve, whether they are anniversaries, travel plans, or personal goals. Ensure that you discuss how to make these future milestones truly meaningful.

Do not underestimate the power of revisiting your shared history while planning for the future; it is vital to strengthen your bond. This practice deepens your connection and enhances your understanding of one another. Reflect on your past experiences and recognize their impact on your relationship. Then, engage in an impactful discussion about your future plans and how they align with your shared vision.

Chapter Nineteen

The Art of Expressing Gratitude

Gratitude is a powerful tool that can significantly strengthen the bond between partners. To effectively express appreciation, make it a daily practice. A heartfelt thank you or a small gesture can go a long way. But it's important to be specific about what you're grateful for—this shows your partner that you genuinely notice their efforts. Consider thoughtful surprises that demonstrate your appreciation, whether it's a handwritten note or a favorite meal. Sharing moments of gratitude fosters an environment of love and positivity, making both partners feel valued. Embrace this practice to deepen your connection and enhance your relationship.

Gratitude Exchange Activity: Reinforce positivity by focusing on what you appreciate about each other.

Instructions: Each partner writes down three things they are grateful for about the other. Example: "I'm grateful for how you supported me last week when I was overwhelmed." Share your lists and discuss how these actions made you feel.

Reflection: How does expressing gratitude enhance your connection and appreciation for each other?

30 Sample Gratitude Statements for Couples

The Gratitude Statements help partners articulate appreciation for each other, fostering a deeper emotional connection.

"I'm so grateful for how you support me when I'm overwhelmed."

"Thank you for making me laugh, even when my day isn't going well."

"I appreciate how you listen to me without judgment."

"I'm so thankful for the little things, like making me coffee in the morning."

"Thank you for believing in me when I doubt myself"

"I'm grateful for your encouraging me to chase my dreams."

"Thank you for your patience when I'm stressed or difficult to be around."

"I appreciate how you always make time for us, even when life gets busy."

"I'm so thankful for how you make me feel loved and cherished daily."

"Thank you for the thoughtful surprises, they always brighten my day."

"I appreciate how you handle challenges with such strength and grace."

"I'm grateful for how safe and comfortable I feel with you."

"Thank you for always knowing exactly what I need."

"I'm so thankful for how you show love to my family and friends."

"I appreciate your sense of humor and how it brings so joy into my life."

"Thank you for being my biggest cheerleader and always rooting for me."

"I'm grateful for how you care for the things I sometimes overlook."

"Thank you for the way you prioritize our relationship—it means so much."

"I appreciate how you make me feel seen and valued for who I am."

"I'm so thankful for your kindness and how you treat others respectfully."

"Thank you for our deep conversations—I feel so connected to you."

"I appreciate how you always find ways to make life exciting and fun."

"I'm grateful for how you inspire me to be a better person daily."

"Thank you for your unwavering love, even during tough times."

"I appreciate you always being willing to compromise to make us happy."

"I'm so thankful for how you've taught me to see the world in new ways."

"Thank you for your honesty and how you trust me with your feelings."

"I appreciate how you handle disagreements with understanding & respect."

"I'm grateful for all the moments of quiet comfort we share."

"Thank you for simply being you—you make my life so much brighter."

How to Use Gratitude Statements?

Utilize the interactive workbook provided in this book for maximum effectiveness. Make it a priority to take turns expressing gratitude daily—do this at dinner or before bed. Furthermore, commit to sharing multiple weekly statements; this intentional gratitude exchange is essential.

Enhance the experience by surprising your partner with gratitude statements written on sticky notes, sent as texts, or delivered as letters. This element of surprise elevates your gratitude practice and adds a meaningful twist.

Chapter Twenty

Love in the Digital Era

Technology is changing how couples communicate, trust, and keep each other close in our hyperconnected society. It might strengthen relationships through intimacy and connectivity, but it also brings new challenges – invisibility, reliance, and distrust. This chapter explores the tension between digital closeness and autonomy, providing practical guidance, tips, and exercises for creating a healthy relationship in the digital world.

Digital intimacy provides unique ways to connect, from messaging to video calls to uploading life experiences on social media. Yet it would help to approach this digital terrain cautiously, for miscommunication and overexposure can create confusion, intrusion, and fear. If couples can play it safe and stay at a moderate level, digital intimacy can be achieved in a way that fosters greater emotional connection.

The 4 Key Aspects of Digital Intimacy

1. Maintain Your Personal Space Online: Digital independence refers to the ability to have your own personal space online while respecting individuality, and it is built on a foundation of trust. This concept allows both partners to lead separate digital lives while still maintaining a meaningful connection. Healthy digital independence is achieved when each individual feels at ease with what they choose to share or not share about their online activities, confident that their partner will respect their privacy. This mutual trust also encourages personal time away from screens and devices, fostering a deep sense of security and confidence in the relationship.

Personal Space Online Exercise: Digital Independence Reflection

Journal Individually: Write about how you feel regarding your digital autonomy.

Examples: *"How much of my online activity do I feel comfortable sharing?",* □ or *"Do I trust my partner to respect my privacy?"*

Share with Your Partner: Discuss your reflections and explore what digital independence means to you both.

Agree on Independence Zones: Examples: *"I'll have private time on social media, but I'm happy to share major updates."* □ or *"We don't need to reply instantly to every text to show we care.*

2. Setting Boundaries – Establishing clear digital boundaries is essential. Without them, technology can create a sense of perpetual "on call" for your partner, which often results in overwhelm and miscommunication. To improve your relationships, set aside specific times to disconnect—such as during meals or before bedtime, allowing you to focus entirely on each other. Limit the frequency of texting or calling. It's crucial to have open discussions about comfort levels when sharing personal relationship information online, ensuring everyone involved feels safe and respected. Creating and respecting digital boundaries is vital for fostering a secure and considerate environment. Respecting individual choices for tagging, posting, or commenting helps to build a stronger understanding and harmony in your connections. Lastly, designate screen-free areas, like dining tables and certain rooms, to encourage meaningful, face-to-face interactions that strengthen your bond.

Setting Boundaries Exercise: Technology-Free Time

Set aside one hour each day to disconnect from your phones and devices. Engage in offline activities like cooking together, playing a board game, or going for a walk. After this break, take the time to discuss its impact on your connection and modify your routine accordingly.

3. Building Digital Trust – Trust in the digital space is not just a necessity, but also a gateway to a more fulfilling and secure relationship. It requires honesty, transparency, and a commitment to avoiding destructive behaviors like secrecy and invasive monitoring. Common trust issues, such as snooping on messages or social media accounts, overanalyzing online interactions, or hiding online behavior, can be overcome with the right approach.

To foster genuine digital trust, you must be transparent and open in your communication. Share your online habits, including who you frequently interact with. Respect personal boundaries and resist the temptation to access your partner's devices without consent. If something online bothers you, voice your feelings calmly. For example, you might say, "When I saw that comment, I felt insecure. Can we discuss it?" This open dialogue is a powerful tool in building trust.

Trust-Building Dialogue Exercise:

Set Aside Time: Arrange a dedicated time to engage with your partner about digital trust. Use these prompts:

"What online behaviors make you feel most loved and secure?"
"What online behaviors make you feel uneasy or undervalued?"

Establish clear agreements on behaviors that will strengthen trust, such as sharing passwords—only if both partners feel comfortable with that—but strictly to enhance trust, not as a means of control.

4. Effective Digital Communication – Technology can bridge physical distances, but it's crucial to recognize that overreliance on texts and calls can lead to misunderstandings. Use messages to express love and check in on one another—not just for logistical purposes. Misunderstandings often stem from tone; if there's any ambiguity in a message, don't hesitate to ask directly, *"What do you mean by that?"*

While technology can enhance connection, you must prioritize face-to-face discussions for serious matters. Make it a habit to send daily texts that transcend logistics, such as:

"I'm thinking of you and appreciate everything you do."□
or *"I'm so proud of you today."*

After sharing these messages, discuss how they made each of you feel and whether they strengthened your connection.

23 Templates for Romantic Letters or Texts

These templates assist couples in expressing their love and appreciation for one another. They are versatile, inspiring notes, texts, or even verbal declarations.

"One thing I admire most about you is how you always..."

"The way you [specific action or quality] makes me feel so lucky to have you."

"If I could describe my favorite memory of us in one word, it would be [word], because..."

"When I think about you, the first thing that makes me smile is..."

"One moment that reminded me how much I love you recently was..."

"If I could relive any day with you, it would be..."

"Every time I see you smile, it reminds me of..."

"I want you to know that even on the hardest days, you make me feel..."

"The moment I knew I wanted to spend my life with you was when..."

"When I think about the future, one thing I'm most excited about with you is..."

"You inspire me every day by..."

"The way you make me laugh when [specific moment] is something I'll never forget."

"I fell in love with you because..., but I stay in love with you because......"

"My favorite little thing you do that always melts my heart is..."

"If I could bottle up one feeling from being with you, it would be [feeling] because..."

"When I wake up next to you, the first thing I think is..."

"I love how you've taught me to see the world differently by......"

"If I could give you anything in the world, it would be [something symbolic] because......"

"How will you support me when [specific moment] made me feel loved and safe."

"If our love were a song, it would be [song or made-up title], because....."

"I never thought I could feel [specific feeling] until I met you."

"Sometimes I watch you when you're not looking and think....."

"If I could spend forever doing one thing with you, it would be.... because....."

Each prompt is open-ended, allowing for unique responses that can be tailored to your relationship. These templates are versatile, focusing on specific moments, qualities, and feelings, and can be used in various forms of communication. Whether you're writing romantic letters, texts, or notes, these prompts can significantly enhance your relationship. They're perfect for deepening your connection and helping you articulate feelings that often go unsaid.

Embracing these strategies and exercises will allow you to turn the digital landscape into a powerful ally for intimacy, ensuring it is a source of closeness rather than a barrier to connection.

Chapter Twenty-One

Milestones in Love

L ife transitions are significant changes or milestones that couples often face together. When navigated with care, communication, and, most importantly, mutual support, these transitions can strengthen a relationship by creating a reassuring and supportive environment. Our lives tend to transition in waves, impacting our relationships along the way. Whether it involves the excitement of a new beginning or the challenges of a major change, learning to cope with these everyday life events can help create deeper bonds. Let's explore how changing times affect our relationships and find ways to move forward together!

Common Life transitions for couples are:

Moving In Together: Adjusting to shared space, habits, and routines.

Marriage: Defining expectations and roles in the long term.

Career Changes: Navigating new jobs, promotions, relocations, or unemployment.

Financial Changes: Manage joint finances, pay off debt, or save.

Parenthood: Adapting to the challenges and joys of raising children.

Empty Nest Syndrome: Redefining the relationship.

Health Issues: Coping with illness, injury, or changes in your health.

Aging and Retirement: Adjusting to life during the aging process.

Loss of a Loved One: Supporting each other through grief.

Blended Families: Navigating relationships with extended families.

Strategies to Navigate Life Transitions

1. Communicate Expectations, Fears, and Hopes: The key to navigating life transitions is open and blame-free communication. Express your feelings using 'I' statements, which helps to avoid assigning blame. For instance, instead of saying, 'You always leave the dishes for me to clean up,' you can say, 'I feel overwhelmed when I have to clean up after dinner alone.' Before moving in together, it's crucial to discuss how to divide household responsibilities and manage finances effectively.

2. Define Success Together: By collaboratively defining success during this transition and breaking goals into small, actionable steps, you empower yourselves. If you're starting a family, it's vital to discuss parenting styles, financial planning, and the division of childcare. A practical step could be researching and agreeing on a budget for baby expenses. This approach gives you a sense of control and direction, making the transition smoother and more manageable.

3. Acknowledge That Change Takes Time: It's important to accept that adjustments may not be smooth initially. Regularly revisiting your plans and adapting as needed is a key strategy. This approach provides reassurance and prepares you for potential changes. For instance, if one partner starts a new job, agree to reassess work-life balance in a few months to ensure that neither partner feels neglected.

4. Prioritize Personal Care: It's crucial to support each other in caring for individual needs while maintaining your connection. By scheduling regular quality time together to nurture intimacy, you show each other that you value and respect your relationship. For example, engage in new hobbies during retirement but also ensure that you pursue individual interests. This balance is key to a healthy and fulfilling life transition.

5. Utilize Your Support Network: Relying on trusted friends, family, or professionals for guidance during life transitions is crucial. Consider couples counseling during particularly challenging times. If you are navigating grief, attend a support group or therapy together to process your emotions. Remember, seeking support is a clear sign of strength, not weakness. It's a way to reassure yourselves that you're not alone in this journey.

Role-Playing Future Scenarios for Couples

Role-playing helps couples prepare for life transitions by exploring potential challenges, practicing communication, and developing strategies together.

How to Use Role-Playing:

1 . Choose a Scenario: Select a life transition you're anticipating or worried about. Examples include moving in together, deciding on retirement plans, or navigating a financial crisis.

2 . Define the context: Where are you, and what is happening? Example: "We've just moved into a new home, and we're figuring out who does what around the house."

3 . Assign Roles: One partner shares their perspective or concern, and the other responds as they might in real life. Switch roles to explore both viewpoints.

4 . Practice Problem-Solving: Act out potential conflicts or decisions and practice resolving them respectfully. For example, "What happens if one of us feels like we're doing more chores than the other?"

5 . Debrief: Discuss how it felt and what you learned after the role-play. Example: "I realized I'd like more clarity on expectations before we start this transition."

Example Scenarios for Role-Playing

Moving in Together Scenario: One partner is concerned about sharing space, while the other is excited. **How to Role-Play:** Discuss boundaries, routines, and how to handle disagreements.

Retirement Scenario: One partner wants to travel, while the other prefers staying home. **How to Role-Play:** Practice a conversation about compromise and shared priorities.

Parenthood Scenario: Discuss how you'll handle sleepless nights, parenting styles, or balancing work and family. **How to Role-Play:** Act out a late-night diaper change scenario or decide how to discipline a child.

Career Relocation Scenario: One partner is offered a job in a new city, but the other hesitates to move. **How to Role-Play:** Discuss the pros and cons and practice communicating your feelings.

Benefits of Role-Playing Life Transitions

Practicing dialogue in a safe, hypothetical space is essential for reducing miscommunication during transitions and building empathy. Understanding your partner's perspective is crucial for fostering connection and collaboration.

Anticipating challenges and solutions empowers couples to feel prepared and effectively reduces anxiety. Engaging in various scenarios reinforces your ability to navigate changes as a united team.

By identifying common life transitions, implementing practical strategies, and utilizing role-playing exercises, couples will significantly strengthen their bond and prepare effectively for the future. This strategic blend of preparation, communication, and teamwork ensures you navigate life's inevitable changes with confidence and ease.

Chapter Twenty-Two

Unconventional Relationships

Have you ever considered just how incredibly diverse the relationship community is? We've transformed our view of relationships from a black-and-white picture into a high-definition projection of love and connection. Explore this vibrant spectrum and see how people interact, embrace, and create together. So buckle up and prepare for an exciting journey into relationship diversity! Before we dive in, let's define "relationship diversity." Simply put, it's the beautiful reality that relationships can take any form we desire. There is no longer a need for everyone to follow the exact blueprint for a relationship. We are now embracing various partnership models, each valid in its way.

Breaking Free from the One-Size-Fits-All Mold

Remember when romances were like old-fashioned TV dinners? Those days are behind us! We now live in an age of relationship buffets, where you can choose what works best for you and your partner(s). Isn't that refreshing? Today, relationships are all about choices. It's like visiting a candy store, picking different ingredients to create your unique blend of love.

Want a multi-partner relationship with a sprinkle of polyamory? Go for it! Interested in a same-sex romance with a spiritual element? That's on the menu too! It's entirely up to you to design a relationship that fits your needs. And with that out of the way, let's look at some of the different types of relationships that are alive and well in the contemporary age. From monogamous relationships to open relationships, from long-distance relationships to LGBTQ+ partnerships, and from polyamorous relationships to asexual relationships, the spectrum of relationship diversity is vast and ever-expanding. Don't get me wrong. This is not an exhaustive list – the thing about relationship diversity is that something new is coming up every single day!

Exploring the Rainbow of Relationship Structures

Polyamorous Relationships: Love Multiplied

Polyamory – not a lingo; it's a different way to love! And what if we were allowed to form romantic relationships with many, varied partners, all with their full knowledge and consent? Sounds complex? Sure, it can be. But to many, it's a way to enjoy love in abundance. Polyamorous relationships can offer a broader support network, interconnecting emotional and physical experiences and empowerment through multi-relationship management. Yet they also carry their baggage: Sharing time and attention with their partners, navigating jealousy and insecurity, and dealing with societal misconceptions.

Long-Distance Relationships: Love Knows No Borders.

Why must you live in the same zip code to be in a relationship? Even long-distance lovers demonstrate that love does not need to travel across distances, time zones, and continents. Technology has made it simpler than ever to stay connected. Ways to thrive with distance include regular video dates, surprise care packages, electronic activities (such as watching movies together), and planning for the future.

LGBTQ+ Partnerships: Love is Love

Lesbian and gay people have long led the way in questioning established relationship structures. Marriages – from the same-sex to those that accommodate trans identity – are a testament to the strength of love in all its forms. LGBTQ+ relationships offer breaking gender stereotypes between couples, redefining family structures, and calling for more acceptance and legal recognition in society.

The Benefits and Flexibility Relationship Diversity

So, now that we've looked at a few different relationship arrangements, you may be thinking, "Why should I do this?" You know what? The benefits of being different in relationships aren't just for the world—they're good for you, too! Embracing relationship diversity can increase empathy, improve communication skills, and lead to a more open-minded approach to life. It can also help you understand and appreciate the unique qualities of your partner (s) and foster a stronger, more resilient relationship.

The more flexible we can be in our relationships, the more capable we are of accepting different styles of relationships. This is like love yoga—you stretch, and you feel stronger! Diverse relationships require the best communication ability. Whether you are negotiating polyamory or communicating across cultural chasms in an intercultural relationship, you'll probably turn into a communication ninja!

Different relationship models bring different insights. This plurality will allow for better problem-solving and conflict resolution—a relationship with the Swiss Army Knife for the win!

Overcoming Challenges in Diverse Relationships

But it's not all rainbows and butterflies, of course. Different relationships can present distinct difficulties. However, fear not – we've got a few tricks to make it through these waters! Overcoming these challenges can make you and your relationships more decisive, resilient, and determined than ever.

Dealing with Societal Judgment

Unfortunately, not everyone has yet been on board with relationship diversity. How do you approach judgment? Surround yourself with people you can trust, share with others when you feel they need it (and it is okay to do so), and do not let others make you think your relationship is less than perfect. Remember, supportive communities are out there waiting for you to join them.

Navigating Legal and Financial Complexity

Managing legal and financial complexities can be challenging in diverse relationship types. Researching your rights and consulting with experts, such as lawyers and financial advisers, when necessary while advocating for legal recognition and safety is crucial.

Embracing Open Conversations about Diversity

The easiest way to celebrate relationship diversity is to talk about it. Let's discuss how to facilitate meaningful conversations about relationship diversity. Open, honest conversations about relationship diversity can help you and your partners feel more connected and understood. Is it time to discuss relationship diversity with your partner(s)? Here are some conversation starters:

"What do you think the perfect relationship is?"
"How do you feel about [a specific relationship pattern]? "
"What would you like to learn or adapt about our relationship? "

Do you want to encourage relationship variation across your more comprehensive network? Consider Running discussion groups or workshops, distributing content on social media, or funding organizations that champion relationship diversity.

Real-Life Stories: Diverse Relationships in Action

Sometimes, the only way to understand diverse relationships is to talk to their bearers. Let's examine some real-world stories that illustrate the appeal of relational diversity.

Maria and Akiko: Bridging Cultures Through LoveMaria, from Brazil, and Akiko, from Japan, met in Canada. They are not just two individuals; they represent three diverse cultures. They are learning a foreign language, blending their holiday customs, and teaching their child to embrace being a global citizen.

The Thompson-Bakers: A Modern FamilyThe Thompson-Bakers are Sarah, Michael, and Lisa, a polygamous duo with two young children. They've built a world of love, understanding, and transparency. They experience challenges—such as how to tell people about their family—but are steadfast in their singular connection—embracing Your Unique Relationship Journey.

Remember, there is no "right" way to be in a relationship. Ultimately, it's all about whether or not your relationship(s) bring you happiness, learning, and satisfaction. You may be married, polyamorous, or happily single, but your position in the world is valid and deserves to be celebrated. As we've learned, relationship diversity isn't an abstract notion—it's a living reality that changes how we love and relate. The more diversity we allow ourselves to enjoy, the more knowledge we gain, and the more genuine collaborations we create, leading to personal growth and empowerment.

So, if you're interested in experimenting with new relationship models or want to appreciate the gorgeous differences around you, always remember this: love is love in all its awesomeness. Be open, speak openly, and love with decency and honesty.

I wish we had a planet where all relationships are celebrated, valued, and allowed to thrive. Every relationship, regardless of its form, deserves to be celebrated. Isn't that what love is?

Chapter Twenty-Three

Final Thoughts and Next Steps

A s we come to the end of this meaningful journey together, take a moment to honestly acknowledge the growth and empowerment you have experienced along the way. We have explored the delicate nuances of emotional and sexual bonding—essential elements that lay the groundwork for lasting, fulfilling relationships. By embracing the principles and techniques we've discussed, you are not merely deepening your love for your partner; you are also gaining the tools to positively shape your relationship's future.

We've witnessed how emotional closeness, grounded in trust, empathy, and vulnerability, creates intimacy, belonging, and a spirit of partnership. Communication is the lifeblood of any connection, and we have worked together on nurturing skills like active listening, making requests, and resolving conflicts compassionately. These skills empower you to express your feelings and needs openly, reducing misunderstandings and cultivating a safe space for you and your partner. By mastering these techniques, you pave the way for meaningful conversations that draw you closer to one another.

It's important to remember that deepening your emotional connection is about more than words. It requires investing time in quality shared experiences and fostering empathetic connections. We've touched upon the importance of intentional moments in your lives—whether that's through meditation, storytelling, or simply being present with one another. These practices nourish the emotional soil in which love and intimacy can blossom.

Exploring the realm of intimacy also calls for creativity and an open heart. We have shared ways to break free from routine, understand each other's desires, and sprinkle joy and playfulness into your connection. By embracing novelty and spontaneity, you can breathe fresh life into your relationship, ensuring your physical bond is as vibrant as your emotional ties.

Creating a nurturing environment based on openness, vulnerability, and healthy boundaries is crucial for a loving relationship. We have discussed how fostering authenticity allows both partners to share their true selves. When you prioritize trust, you build a partnership rooted in respect and reliability, creating a safe haven for both of you.

While relationship challenges can be daunting, they also present significant opportunities for growth together. We've reviewed strategies to manage emotional triggers, align sexual needs, and ensure that your relationship coexists harmoniously with other life commitments. With these tools, you can approach challenges with resilience, turning struggles into valuable learning experiences, ultimately strengthening your dedication to nurturing your relationship.

Self-discovery is a beautiful, ongoing journey. By reflecting on your feelings, understanding each other's attachment styles, and supporting growth, you can forge a deeper, more resilient bond. This commitment to personal and shared growth will profoundly enhance your relationship.

Long-term intimacy requires consistent effort and a touch of creativity. Daily intention and openness to new experiences make your relationship feel fresh and invigorating. By continuously infusing new life and meaning into your connection, your love can endure and flourish through every season of life.

Here are some points to take away:

1. Prioritize communication and active listening in your relationship.
2. Invest time to build strong connections and create meaningful experiences together.
3. Establish trust through openness, transparency, and respect.
4. Make your sexual relationship enjoyable and exciting.
5. Address issues with empathy and a focus on problem-solving.
6. Support each other's growth and improvement.
7. Plan for the future together, sharing a common purpose and vision.

Embrace these suggestions with an open heart, and remember that the journey toward a deeper, more intimate connection—both sexual and emotional—is a beautiful and ongoing process.

I warmly encourage you to begin incorporating these practices into your relationship. Whether you choose to express your love through small, simple gestures or more grand and elaborate ones, each step you take is a meaningful contribution to strengthening your bond. Thank you for allowing me to be part of this journey with you, and for considering these ideas to enrich your life together.

I am here to support you as you navigate this path. The journey to intimacy can be a joyful experience, filled with moments of ease and connection. With genuine effort and commitment, you and your partner can nurture a flourishing relationship filled with love, trust, and happiness. Continue to embrace, cherish, and nurture the unique love you share with one another.

Make a Difference with Your Review

USA REVIEW PAGE

"Great opportunities to help others seldom come, but small ones surround us every day."-- Sally Koch

Giving without expecting anything back makes our lives brighter and helps others in ways we might never see. Right now, you have a chance to do just that. **Will you help someone you don't know if it costs you nothing and you don't get credit for it?**

That "someone" could be a person who feels stuck, worried, or confused about how to talk with their partner. They might need this book to find hope and new ideas. But first, they must see that this book is worth their time. That's where your review can help.

Your Review Makes a Significant Difference

Most people look at a book's cover and reviews before reading it. By sharing your thoughts, you can guide others and show them how this book can improve their relationships. Your review could be the deciding factor for someone needing this book, making you a powerful influencer in their decision-making process. **Leaving a review is a quick and easy way to**

make a difference. It takes less than 60 seconds, but its impact can last a lifetime. Your contribution, though small in time, is significant and valuable.

Your honest feedback might inspire someone you'll never meet. You can leave your review on popular bookstores or websites like Amazon or Goodreads. Click the link below to leave your review. Even a few words can mean the world to someone searching for better communication methods. Please take a moment to leave your review now.

UK REVIEW PAGE

If you enjoy helping a stranger just by sharing your thoughts, welcome to the club! I appreciate your support in spreading the word about "Stress-Free Communication Skills for Couples:"

Thank you so much for being part of this mission. Now, let's return to learning how to build closer, happier partnerships—one simple step at a time.

Your biggest fan, **Sophia Simone**

P.S. Sending a copy of this book to someone who needs it is another way to share kindness. It might be the start of a positive change in their life.

P.P.S. If you want your review to stand out, consider adding a photo—maybe the cover or a favorite page. Your picture and a few words of praise can touch the hearts of many. Thank you for being part of this journey!

Chapter Twenty-Four

References

Active listening in relationships: A path to deeper intimacy. (n.d.). Holding Hope MFT. Retrieved from https://holdinghopemft.com/active-listening-a-key-to-deeper-intimacy-and-understanding-in-your-relationship/

Building a strong foundation and trust in romantic relationships. (n.d.). Yana Kazekamp Blog. Retrieved from https://www.yanakazekamp.com/blog/building-strong-foundation-trust-romantic-relationships

Co-regulating for couples: Techniques for stress relief. (n.d.). Couples Learn. Retrieved from https://coupleslearn.com/coregulating-for-couples/

Daily rituals of connection. (n.d.). Gottman Institute. Retrieved from https://www.gottman.com/blog/3-daily-rituals-that-stop-spouses-from-taking-each-other-for-granted/

Effective communication strategies for couples. (n.d.). Epic Counseling Solutions. Retrieved from https://epiccounselingsolutions.com/effectiv e-communication-strategies-for-couples-a-therapists-guide/

Emotional intimacy: The key to a resilient and fulfilling relationship. Retrieved from https://www.psychologytoday.com/us/blog/the-discomfo rt-zone/202408/emotional-intimacy-the-key-to-a-resilient-and-fulfilling

Emotional safety is necessary for emotional connection. (n.d.). Gottman Institute. Retrieved from https://www.gottman.com/blog/emotional-s afety-is-necessary-for-emotional-connection/

Five stages of intimacy. (2021, July 14). Vivian Baruch. Retrieved from https://vivianbaruch.com/2021/07/14/five-stages-of-intimacy-2/

Four principles behind emotional triggers in relationships. (n.d.). Judy Wilkins-Smith. Retrieved from https://judywilkins-smith.com/four-pr inciples-behind-emotional-triggers-in-relationships/

How attachment styles influence romantic relationships. (n.d.). Columbia Psychiatry. Retrieved from https://www.columbiapsychiatry.org/ne ws/how-attachment-styles-influence-romantic-relationships

How emotional intelligence impacts an intimate relationship. Retrieved from https://www.psychologytoday.com/us/blog/overcoming-destruc tive-anger/202410/how-emotional-intelligence-impacts-an-intimate

How playfulness can transform your love life. (2023, December). Psychology Today. Retrieved from https://www.psychologytoday.com/us/blog/everyone-on-top/20 2312/how-playfulness-can-transform-your-love-life

How to feel comfortable expressing sexual desires with your partner. (n. d.). Gottman Institute. Retrieved from https://www.gottman.com/blo g/how-to-feel-comfortable-expressing-sexual-desires-with-your-partner/

How to talk about difficult subjects in your relationship. (n.d.). Eugene Therapy. Retrieved from https://eugenetherapy.com/article/how-to-talk -about-difficult-subjects-in-your-relationship/

How to use mindfulness to strengthen your relationships. (n.d.). Gottman Institute. Retrieved from https://www.gottman.com/blog/how-to-use -mindfulness-to-strengthen-your-relationships

"I" statements: How to use them & examples. (n.d.). Thriveworks. Re- trieved from https://thriveworks.com/help-with/communication/i-stat ements/

Reliability and consistency: The pillars of trustworthiness. (2024, March 2 6) . https://www.erikalabuzanlopeztherapy.com/blog-psychotherapy-marria ge-counseling-infertility-postpartum-depression-minimalism-leaguecity -houston-tx/2024/3/26/reliability-and-consistency-the-pillars-of-trustwo rthiness

Social bonding through shared experiences: The role of … (n.d.). Royal Society Publishing. Retrieved from https://royalsocietypublishing.org/d oi/10.1098/rsos.240048

The art of compromise: Balancing individual needs in a relationship. (n. d.). Arrival Counseling. Retrieved from https://www.arrivalcs.com/blog /the-art-of-compromise-balancing-individual-needs-in-a-relationship

Trust, safety, and respect: The importance of boundaries. (n.d.). Stanford University Student Affairs. Retrieved from https://studentaffairs.stanfor d.edu/how-life-treeting-you-importance-of-boundaries

33 couples therapy exercises, activities & questions. (n.d.). CarePatron. Retrieved from [https://www.carepatron.com/guides/couples-therapy-e xercises](https://www.carepatron.com/guides/couples-therapy-exercises)

109 fun date night ideas to inspire romance. (n.d.). The Knot. Retrieved from https://www.theknot.com/content/date-ideas

15 relationship milestones that are worth celebrating. (n.d.). Marriage.com. Retrieved from [https://www.marriage.com/advice/relationship/relationship-milestones-that-are-worth-celebrating/]

15 tips for building resilient relationships. (n.d.). Marriage.com. Retrieved from [https://www.marriage.com/advice/relationship/resilient-relationships/]

17 reasons why quality time in a relationship is important. (n.d.). Marriage.com. Retrieved from https://www.marriage.com/advice/relationship/relationships-need-quality-time

5 best couples therapy exercises for a stronger relationship. (n.d.). Holding Hope MFT. Retrieved from https://holdinghopemft.com/5-therapist-recommended-couples-exercises-for-a-stronger-relationship/

5 effective communication techniques for couples. (n.d.). Counselling in Melbourne. Retrieved from (https://www.counsellinginmelbourne.com.au/communication-techniques-for-couples/)

Made in United States
Troutdale, OR
03/20/2025

29910519R00076